RUTH
—
DAVID
—
FRIENDSHIP

Group's
hands-On
BiBLE
curriculum™

Grades 1 and 2
Fall
Teacher Guide

Group

Loveland, Colorado

Group

Hands-On Bible Curriculum™, Grades 1 and 2, Fall
Copyright © 1994, 1996, and 1998 Group Publishing, Inc.

First printing, 1998

Credits
Contributing Authors: Judy Brown, Lori Haynes Niles, and Beth Rowland Wolf
Editors: Beth Rowland Wolf, Lois Keffer, and Jan Kershner
Managing Editor: Paul Woods
Chief Creative Officer: Joani Schultz
Copy Editor: Candace McMahan
Art Director: Jean Bruns
Cover Art Director: Janet Barker
Cover Designers: Janet Barker and Helen H. Lannis
Designers: Dori Walker and Jean Bruns
Computer Graphic Artist: Rosalie Lawrence
Cover Photographer: Jafe Parsons
Illustrators: RoseAnne Buerge, Vicki Logan, and Jennifer Skopp
Audio Engineer: Steve Saavedra
Production Manager: Peggy Naylor

ISBN 0-7644-0092-4
Printed in the United States of America.

CONTENTS

H·O·W T·O U·S·E T·H·I·S B·O·O·K

 ## WHY HANDS-ON BIBLE CURRICULUM™?

There's nothing more exciting than helping children develop a relationship with God. But teaching first- and second-graders about God can be a challenge. It's difficult to find activities that work with readers and nonreaders. It's hard to explain abstract truths that many adults may not understand. Some children have been in church since birth and appear to know it all. For others, learning about God is brand-new. Teachers tell us they're desperate for something that works.

We've found a way to get children excited to learn about God. Each quarter of Hands-On Bible Curriculum™ is packed with fresh, creative, *active* programming that will capture children's interest and make them eager for more.

Here's why Hands-On Bible Curriculum will work for you.

 ## A NEW APPROACH TO LEARNING

Research shows that children remember about 90 percent of what they *do* but less than 10 percent of what they *hear.* What does this say to us? Simply that children don't learn by being lectured! They need to be actively involved in lively experiences that bring home the lesson's point.

Group's Hands-On Bible Curriculum uses a unique approach to Christian education called active learning. In each session, children participate in a variety of fun and memorable learning experiences that help them understand one important point. As each activity unfolds, children discover and internalize Bible stories and biblical truths. Because they're *doing* instead of just listening, children remember what they learn.

Your children will be fascinated with the neat gadgets and gizmos packed in the Learning Lab®. And you'll feel good about seeing children grow spiritually while they're having fun.

To build excitement, keep the contents of the Learning Lab under cover. Children will be curious about what wonderful gizmos will appear in next week's lesson.

All the activities are designed to work with classes of any size, although we recommend having at least one teacher for every 10 children. The items in the Learning Lab may be used in several lessons, so be sure to hang on to them.

In each lesson you'll find a photocopiable "Growing Together" handout to send home with children. Besides providing an important link between home and church, the "Growing Together" handout features great art projects, family activities, prayers, and parenting tips to help parents reinforce the point of the lesson at home. You can encourage parents' involvement during the next 13 weeks by mailing photocopies of the parents letter found on page 11. All the pages in the Teacher Guide are perforated to make your job easier. Just tear out the photocopiable pages and make as many photocopies as you need for your class.

The items listed below are typical supplies that may be used in the lessons in this book. All other items required for teaching are included in the Learning Lab. We recommend your children use their own Bibles in this course so they can discover for themselves the value and relevance of the Scriptures.

- cassette player
- chalkboard and chalk
- construction paper
- crayons
- glue or glue stick
- index cards
- markers
- masking tape
- newsprint
- old magazines
- old newspaper
- paper clips
- paper cups
- pencils
- plain paper
- scissors
- snacks
- stapler
- transparent tape
- trash cans

SUCCESSFUL TEACHING: YOU CAN DO IT!

What does active learning mean to you as a teacher? It takes a lot of pressure off because the spotlight shifts from you to the children. Instead of being the principal player, you become a guide and facilitator—a choreographer of sorts! This doesn't mean that you "check out" from teaching. It's your job to guide children to The Point of the lesson. These ideas will get you started in your new role:

● **Be creative in your use of classroom space.** Move your tables aside so children can move around freely and work in groups. Have chairs available but be willing to sit on the floor as well. Chairs can be a distraction, and moving them around slows down your lesson.

● **Think about open areas in the church.** These places might be available for activities: the foyer, the front of the sanctuary, a side yard, or the parking lot. Children love variety; a different setting can bring new life and excitement to your lessons.

● **Be sure to help children tie each experience to The Point of the lesson.** Every activity in each lesson is designed to teach a specific point. It's important to repeat The Point over and over during the lesson to make sure children hear it and learn it.

Studies show that people need to hear new information up to 75 times to learn it. You may think you're being redundant, but you're actually reinforcing The Point and making sure children see how it applies to their lives. Whenever you can during the lesson, repeat The Point just as it's worded. You can even have the children say it with you to make sure they know it.

● **Remember that the gizmos from the Learning Lab are exciting to children.** Keep distractions to a minimum by gathering the gizmos before class discussions.

● **Focus on discussing the activities with children.** Don't skip over the discussion in favor of doing more activities. The activities allow children to *experience* biblical truths. And the discussions teach children how to *apply* the experiences to their lives. The printed discussion questions and summary statements will help children explore their feelings, discover important biblical principles, and decide how to apply these principles to their lives. But if your class is large, don't think every child must answer every question. Children will learn from those who share even if only two or three answer each question.

● **Ask—don't tell.** As you lead discussions with your class, ask open-ended questions rather than rephrasing questions as statements and asking children to agree. Your children will learn much more about God if they make the discoveries about the Bible themselves. Trust the Holy Spirit to teach them.

● **Read the suggested responses.** With each discussion question, we've included answers your children might give. These aren't meant to tell you what the "right" answers are but simply to prepare you for what children might say. Don't worry if children give "wrong" answers. They need to have freedom to explore. They'll learn from the answers other children give.

● **Don't forget to use active listening.** Ask, "What did you mean?" Say, "Tell me more." These techniques will cause children to explore their beliefs and learn more about God. They'll also give you a chance to get to know children better and find out what they know.

● **Keep children excited with the Learning Lab gizmos.** Children are intrigued by the items we've chosen to show them how Scripture is relevant to their lives. Keep children interested by showing the Learning Lab items only as each one is used in the lessons. This way, there will be a new and exciting discovery each week.

● **Remember that children learn in different ways.** So don't shy away from an activity just because you've never done anything like it before. It may be just what's needed to help one of your children get The Point.

● **Get to know your children.** When you meet your class members for the first time, get to know them by name. Ask a fun question such as "If you were an animal, what would you be and why?" to help everyone get to know one another.

And when new children show up from week to week, welcome them to the class and help them feel at home. Your sincere interest in each class member will greatly enhance the experiences you'll share in the next 13 weeks.

● **Know your children's abilities and needs.** Refresh your memory about what it is like to be a first- or second-grader by scanning the chart on page 10. It will help you know a bit more about the needs, wants, and abilities of the children you'll be teaching during the next 13 weeks. Be sensitive to children with special needs. Check with parents to see how best to help them. Remind kids that all believers are part of the family of God and have special abilities to offer.

● **Make your class a "safe zone" for children with special needs and learning disabilities.** Avoid calling on children to read or pray aloud if they find it embarrassing. Pair good readers with nonreaders, and both will benefit.

● **Capitalize on your children's strengths.** A student who doesn't read well may be a terrific song leader for your class. A shy, introverted student may have wonderful insights and the ability to resolve problems. When you're forming groups, put active children with quiet, thoughtful children. Learn to let your children shine by drawing on their strengths and allowing each of them to make positive contributions to the class.

● **One of your strongest teaching tools is affirmation.** Children need to know that their contributions are important. Call children by name. Recognize their strengths. Compliment them for Christlike behavior.

● **Try pairing children who know the Bible with children who don't know the Bible.** Let them teach each other. If children know a Bible story so well they lose interest while you tell it, turn the tables and have them teach *you* the Bible story. You might be surprised at how much they know.

● **Let children teach each other.** Don't hesitate to have children work together in small groups for discussions and projects. They'll learn valuable skills to help them work with others. And often, what they learn about God sticks in their minds better when they've learned it from a classmate. The teachers guide gives you many opportunities to have students work in small groups, but use this technique any time to teach children to express their faith to one another.

● **Wait at least 30 seconds for children to respond when you ask a question.** Try offering a controversial answer to spark more responses. Or tell your children to take a few seconds to think of their answers, then call on one child by name to begin the discussion.

● **If your children can't seem to stop talking,** use the attention-getting signal, then tell children it's time to wrap up the discussion and move on.

● **If your children seem restless, take a break.** Burn up their excess energy with action songs or jumping jacks. Then lead a few stretches and return to the lesson. For more ideas, try *Fidget Busters: 101 Quick Attention-Getters for Children's Ministry.* It's available from Group Publishing, P.O. Box 481, Loveland, CO 80539.

● **Be aware of the attitudes children bring into class.** Some children may walk in after fighting with their siblings or being reprimanded by their parents. Encourage them to share their feelings, then be patient as they work to overcome their bad day.

ATTENTION, PLEASE!

Stand back and get ready for a radical idea: Noise can be a good thing in Sunday school! Educators will tell you that children process new information best by interacting with each other. Having quiet and controlled children doesn't necessarily mean your class is a success. A better clue might be seeing happy, involved, excited children moving around the classroom, discussing how to apply to their lives the new truths they're learning.

There is a difference between good and bad noise. Good noise is learning noise—children discovering and sharing new insights. Bad noise is disruptive and destructive. Put an end to bad noise by using the attention-getting signal and separating students who egg each other on.

If noise and activity can be good, how does a teacher keep control?

Good question! And we've got some good answers.

● **Keep things moving!** Most children have about a seven-minute attention span—the amount of time between TV commercials. That means you need to be ready to move on to the next activity *before* children get bored with the current one.

● **Establish attention-getting signals.** Flashing the lights or raising your hand will let children know it's time to stop what they're doing and look at you. You'll find a suggestion for a signal in the introduction to each module. You can use this signal throughout all 13 weeks. Rehearse the signal with your children at the beginning of each class. Once your children become familiar with the signal, regaining their attention will become an automatic classroom ritual.

● **Participate—don't just observe.** Your enthusiasm will draw children into an activity and help them see you as a person, not just someone in authority. Get down to children's eye level so they don't think of you as a giant but as an accessible, caring friend.

● **Look for teachable moments.** Sometimes an activity will look like it didn't work. Or maybe something entirely unexpected will happen. But children can learn from an activity that seems to have flopped. It may actually provide a wonderful opportunity for learning if you ask questions such as "Why didn't this work out?" "How is this like what happens in real life?" or "What can we learn from this experience?"

● **Adjust the lessons for your class.** When options are given, use one or both of them. Use the Bonus Ideas beginning on page 155 to lengthen the lesson. You can also use the Out-of-the-Box Ideas that are listed in some lessons to lengthen a class session. These ideas require supplies that aren't included in the Learning Lab. Each lesson is complete without the Out-of-the-Box Ideas, but these extras are lots of fun when you want to do something more.

The lessons can also be shortened. If you have a large group or a short class session, pick three or four of the activities that will work best with your children. If you make The Point during each activity, you'll have taught something significant even if you don't get through the whole lesson.

● **If you're running short on time, skip to the closing.** Every activity teaches biblical truths, but the closing usually includes prayer and a commitment to action. The closing activity will solidify the lesson's Point and provide a wrap-up for the lesson.

● **Adapt the lessons to your class size.** While each activity works with larger classes, the bigger the class size, the more time the activity will take. But don't worry; children will get the main point in every activity. They'll have caught the lesson aim even if they don't do every activity.

● **Use the Fidget Buster.** It's a lively activity designed to help children burn up excess energy then settle down quickly and focus on the lesson.

● **Use the Time Stuffers.** These independent-learning activities will keep children occupied (and learning!)

✔ when they arrive early,

✔ when an individual or a group finishes an activity before the others, or

✔ when there is extra time after the lesson.

You'll find a Time Stuffer in the introduction to each module. After a quick setup, children can use the activity during all the lessons of the four- or five-week module.

You can also stretch your teaching time by doing one of the options you skipped earlier or by picking up one of the Bonus Ideas beginning on page 155.

● **You may want to write each lesson's outline and discussion questions on newsprint or a chalkboard.** This is a great way to prepare the lesson, and it will allow you to interact with the children instead of keeping your nose in the Teacher Guide. An added benefit is that children who read will have time to think about their answers.

● **Include time for Remembering God's Word.** The Key Verse found in the introduction to each module will help you emphasize God's Word each week. Fun, active memory-verse activities will help children hide God's Word in their hearts and apply it to their lives in a way that will really make a difference. And look for the Key Verse Connection and Bible Insight in the margin of each lesson. The Key Verse Connection will help you tie the module's Key Verse to The Point of the lesson, and the Bible Insight will add depth to your Bible study.

● **Rely on the Holy Spirit to help you.** Don't be afraid of children's questions. Remember, the best answers are those the children find themselves—not the ones teachers spoon-feed them.

UNDERSTANDING YOUR FIRST- AND SECOND-GRADERS

MENTAL DEVELOPMENT
- Are interested in concrete learning experiences such as dramatizations and rhythms.
- Have a limited concept of time and space; are interested in the present but not in the past or future.
- Yearn for competence in developing skills.

PHYSICAL DEVELOPMENT
- Have high energy levels, which demand a lot of physical activity such as jumping and running.
- Are industrious; like to make things and complete projects.
- Are more interested in the finished product than the process.
- Are developing small-muscle coordination; are beginning to write.

SOCIAL DEVELOPMENT
- Usually prefer to stick to same-sex friendships.
- Thrive on organized games and group activities.
- Want to please teachers but are beginning to recognize their role in relation to their peers.
- Want to win and always be first; have a strong sense of competition with others.

EMOTIONAL DEVELOPMENT
- Express feelings with physical action.
- Crave individual attention and affirmation.
- Are self-centered; each child wants to be first.
- Need to feel capable; this is directly related to their self-esteem.
- Want everything to be fair; have a clear-cut sense of justice.

SPIRITUAL DEVELOPMENT
- Understand God's love and God's world through personal experience.
- Don't comprehend the spiritual nature of God; think of God as a giant, a magician, or an invisible man.
- Don't comprehend the Bible's chronology except that the Old Testament came before Jesus and the New Testament talks about Jesus.
- Have a literal and concrete understanding of Bible stories and biblical truths; don't comprehend abstract ideas such as the Trinity.

GROWING TOGETHER

Dear Parent,

I'm so glad to be your child's teacher this quarter. With our Hands-On Bible Curriculum™, your child will look at the Bible in a whole new way.

For the next 13 weeks, we'll explore what Scripture has to say to first- and second-graders about Ruth, David, and friendship. Using active-learning methods and a surprising assortment of gadgets and gizmos (such as Wikki Stix™, a "super bouncing wheel," and a "squirty fish"), we'll help children discover meaningful applications of God's Word.

Our Hands-On Bible Curriculum welcomes you to play an important part in what your child learns. **Each week children will receive a "Growing Together" handout to take home and share.** "Growing Together" features parenting tips, songs, crafts, prayers, and other activities to help you reinforce the Bible story and the point of each week's lesson.

Let me encourage you to use the "Growing Together" handout regularly; it's a great tool for promoting positive interaction and healthy communication in your family.

Sincerely,

Get FREE TEACHING TIPS for Group's Hands-On Bible Curriculum™

To help make your teaching more effective, Group is providing MinistryNet™, our free online service. With this service, you'll get:

- Helpful teacher ideas for each module.
- Access to a message board with other teachers of Hands-On Bible Curriculum™.
- Plus, all the other timesaving MinistryNet helps for your children's and youth ministries.

In order to use this service, you'll need your own Internet access plus a World Wide Web browser that supports Java™ script and applets. We recommend the newest version of Microsoft Internet Explorer or Netscape Navigator. You can download these browsers from their websites if you do not already have one installed.

Once you have the necessary items above, use your browser to connect to Group Publishing's website at http://www.grouppublishing.com. You can then click on the button for MinistryNet and look for a button that will allow you to set up your free Hands-On Bible Curriculum service.

Then log into MinistryNet and begin to connect with other Hands-On Bible Curriculum teachers and get timely Teacher Tips for your lessons.

Tame the Web
http://www.grouppublishing.com

A unique feature of Group's website is MinistryNet, a subscription service that was created two years ago to provide children's, youth, and adult workers with the most complete library of active-learning ideas, programming, and resources on the Internet. Leaders can access hundreds of games, skits, crowdbreakers, ready-to-go meetings, message boards, chat areas, links to other ministries, clip art, back issues of Group's three magazines, trend information, job listings, prayer requests—and the list goes on!

R·U·T·H

The story of Ruth, Naomi, and Boaz is a quiet account that almost gets lost between the battle victories of Israel's judges and the exciting emergence of a new monarchy. Ruth is a short, simple book about real people who loved God, honored their duties, and held one another in the highest esteem. They valued the traditions that let people hold on to their dignity even when they were down on their luck. Most of all, Ruth, Naomi, and Boaz were careful to please God as they cared for one another's needs, and they were quick to give glory to God when their needs were met. God rewarded these quiet, sincere followers with an amazing gift: Ruth and Boaz were parents to Obed, the father of Jesse, the root from which Christ, the new branch, grew.

This is just the sort of heartwarming kinship your children need to witness and learn from. Ruth's example can help them develop a strong sense of fellowship so they can form healthy friendships with other Christians. Your children will learn how important it is to be loyal to family and friends. They will develop generosity. They will learn to seek counsel with godly men and women. And they will learn the importance of honesty and integrity in daily living. These lessons will help your children live the fulfilling, abundant life that God promises to his people.

FOUR LESSONS ON RUTH

LESSON	PAGE	THE POINT	THE BIBLE BASIS
1—FAITHFUL AND LOYAL	17	God wants us to be loyal to our family and friends.	Ruth 1:1-16
2—WHAT'S MINE IS...	29	God wants us to be generous.	Ruth 2:1-23
3—LISTEN UP	39	Good advice can help us follow God.	Ruth 3:1-15
4—I PROMISE!	49	God wants us to keep our promises.	Ruth 4:1-15

HE SIGNAL

During the lessons on Ruth, your attention-getting signal will be to clap your hands three times. Have children respond by clapping their hands three times and focusing their attention on you. Tell children about this signal before the lesson begins. Explain that it's important to respond to this signal quickly so the class can do as many fun activities as possible.

HE FIDGET BUSTER

LEARNING LAB

When your students are too antsy to pay attention to the lesson, play this gleaning game to get the wiggles out.

Put the *plastic monkeys, felt strips,* and *plastic rings* into the lid of the Learning Lab box. If you have more than 15 children in your class, use paper scraps as well. Have the children stand along one wall.

Say: **In biblical times, farmers left some of their grain in the fields for poor people to glean, or pick up. I'll pretend to be a worker in the fields, gathering the crops. While I'm gathering my crops, I'll leave some grain in the fields for you, the gleaners. When I say "go," your job will be to crawl on your hands and knees and glean as much as you can, as quickly as you can.**

Quickly and carefully fling the items so they're scattered all over the floor. Say: **Ready? Go!**

When everything has been gleaned from the floor, have the children return the items to the box. Say: **Now we can rest from our hard work and enjoy a snack.** Reward the children's hard work with raisins or small pieces of candy. Then return to your lesson.

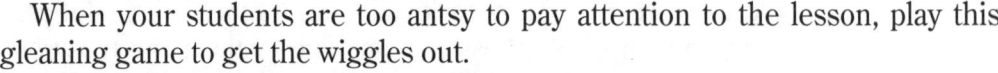HE TIME STUFFER

The Time Stuffer for the four lessons on Ruth is an art project in which children glean their supplies from the room. Stock an area with items from the list of classroom supplies on page 5. This is your chance to clean out your classroom cupboards! Set out any other available supplies that could be used in an art project.

Explain to the children what "gleaning" is. Then, when the children get to class early or finish a project before others do, encourage them to glean art supplies from those you've set out and create their own unique collages or sculptures.

EMEMBERING GOD'S WORD

Each four- or five-week module focuses on a Key Bible Verse. The Key Verse for this module is "Sow for yourselves righteousness, reap the fruit of unfailing love, and break up your unplowed ground; for it is time to seek the Lord, until he comes and showers righteousness on you" **(Hosea 10:12).**

This module's Key Verse will teach children that God is growing good things in their lives. Look for the Key Verse Connection in the margin of each lesson. It will help you tie the module's Key Verse to The Point of the lesson. Have fun using these ideas any time during the lessons on Ruth.

HARVESTING GOODNESS

Read **Hosea 10:12** aloud. Have the children say the verse with you. Say: **When we plant good deeds in our hearts, enjoy being loyal to our family and friends, and learn new things, God will water us with his goodness. Let's play a fun game to help us remember this Bible verse.** Form teams of four for a relay game. Have the teams line up on one side of the room. Mark a finish line on the opposite side of the room.

The first person on each team skips across the room, pretends to dig a hole, skips back, and tags the second person in line. The second person skips across the room, pretends to plant flower seeds, skips back, and tags the third person in line. The third person skips across the room, pretends to water the seeds, skips back, and tags the fourth person in line. The fourth person skips across the room, pretends to pick the flowers, and skips back. The first team to finish wins.

After the game, ask:
● **What kinds of things would God like to plant in you?** (Kindness; love; being nice to people.)

Say: **When we let God plant his goodness in us, we'll grow more beautiful than the most beautiful flower. Let's say the Bible verse together one more time.** Lead children in repeating the Key Verse.

GOD'S GIFTS

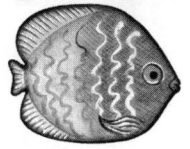

You'll need a glass of water, the *squirty fish* from the Learning Lab, and a sunny churchyard or parking lot.

Take the children outside, and have them stand in a line so that they can see their shadows in front of them. Read **Hosea 10:12.** Have children repeat the verse with you. Ask:
● **What happens to plants when we give them water?** (They grow; they're healthy.)
● **What kinds of goodness do you think God will pour on you?** (Love; friendship; peace; money.)

Say: **The good things that God gives are things that will help us grow—things like love, wisdom, patience, and gentleness. Take a look at the person standing to your right. Think of something God has given that person that will help him or her grow. Each of you will have a chance to fill the** *squirty fish* **with water and squirt the water on your neighbor's shadow. As you squirt the water, you'll say, "God has poured the gift of** _____ **on you."**

Have the first child in line squeeze the air out of the *squirty fish,* submerge it in the glass of water, and release it so that it fills up with water. Then have the first child squeeze the water onto the next child's shadow and complete the sentence. Stand nearby so the children won't be as tempted to squirt each other. Have the last child in the line affirm the child at the beginning of the line.

Then say: **God is causing great things to grow in each of you. Soon it will be time to harvest all these wonderful gifts.** Read the Key Verse again and let children repeat it. Close by thanking God for pouring goodness on us like water.

F·A·I·T·H·F·U·L
A·N·D L·O·Y·A·L

THE POINT
God wants us to be loyal to our family and friends.

THE BIBLE BASIS: 📖
Ruth 1:1-16. Ruth stays with Naomi.

Ruth showed uncommon loyalty when she chose to travel with Naomi to a new home in Bethlehem. In Moab, she was in a familiar culture with people she knew. As a young widow, her family would care for her until she found a new husband. Her fate was less certain in Israel. Moabite women were scorned by Israelite society because when the Israelites were conquering Canaan, Moabite women seduced Israelite warriors and persuaded them to offer sacrifices to Chemosh, the Moabite god. Ruth took a great risk to live in a land where her people weren't trusted. Even though she knew she could be an easy target for mistreatment and abuse, she adopted Naomi as her family, the Israelites as her people, and Israel's God as her God.

While children are naturally loyal, they can still learn from Ruth's example of ardent loyalty. First- and second-graders are eager to please, and they're more than willing to pattern themselves after their heroes down to the last detail. Unfortunately, it's easier for children to copy the outward dress and actions of TV characters than it is to adopt the inward character strengths of Bible superstars such as Ruth and Naomi. Use this lesson to teach children to follow the example of these quiet people who followed God every day. Teach them to be loyal to their families, to their friends, and to God.

Other Scriptures used in this lesson are **Joshua 23:8; John 15:9, 12;** and **Galatians 6:10.**

KEY VERSE
for Lessons 1–4

"Sow for yourselves righteousness, reap the fruit of unfailing love, and break up your unplowed ground; for it is time to seek the Lord, until he comes and showers righteousness on you" (Hosea 10:12).

GETTING THE POINT

Children will

- find that being loyal means they can be counted on,
- discover that loyalty is sticking by someone no matter what, and
- find out what it means to be a true-blue friend and promise to be that kind of friend.

Before the lesson, collect the items from the Learning Lab for the activities you plan to use. Refer to the pictures in the margin to see what each item looks like.

THIS LESSON AT A GLANCE

SECTION	MINUTES	WHAT CHILDREN WILL DO	LEARNING LAB SUPPLIES	CLASSROOM SUPPLIES
WELCOME TIME	up to 5	**Welcome!**—Receive a warm welcome from the teacher and make name tags.		"In the Fields Name Tags" (p. 25), scissors, markers, tape or safety pins
ATTENTION GRABBER	up to 10	**Always Loyal**—Find a predictable pattern they can count on and see that being loyal means being dependable.	Feather ball	
BIBLE EXPLORATION & APPLICATION	up to 10	**Ruth and Naomi**—Hear the story of Ruth, Naomi, and Orpah from Ruth 1:1-16 and learn that being loyal means being ready to help those they love.		Bible
	up to 10	**Spider-Web Tag**—Play a game in which they have to stick to each other to avoid being tagged and learn from Galatians 6:10 that being loyal means being ready to help.		Bible, masking tape
	up to 15	**True-Blue Friends**—Discuss what true-blue friends would do in specific situations, learn from John 15:9, 12 that being loyal means loving others as Jesus does, and promise to be true-blue friends.		Bible, blue drink-mix or gelatin, water, bowls, "True-Blue" handouts (p. 26), paper towels, pencils
CLOSING	up to 10	**Stick Together**—Learn that being loyal means sticking together through thick and thin and read Joshua 23:8 to learn that God wants them to hold fast to him.	Wikki Stix™	Bible

Remember to make photocopies of the "Growing Together" handout (p. 27) to send home with your children. "Growing Together" is a valuable tool for helping first- and second-graders talk with their parents about what they're learning in class.

T·H·E L·E·S·S·O·N

ELCOME TIME

WELCOME!
(up to 5 minutes)

- Greet each child individually with an enthusiastic smile.
- Thank each child for coming to class today.
- Say: **Today we're going to learn that ⭐ God wants us to be loyal to our family and friends.**
- Help children make name tags. Photocopy the "In the Fields Name Tags" (p. 25), and follow the instructions.
- Tell children that the attention-getting signal you'll use during this lesson is clapping your hands three times. Ask children to respond by clapping their hands three times and focusing their attention on you. Rehearse the signal with the children, telling them to respond quickly so you'll have plenty of time for all the fun activities planned for this lesson.

THE POINT ⭐

ATTENTION GRABBER

ALWAYS LOYAL
(up to 10 minutes)

Show children the *feather ball*. Say: **When you bounce this ball against the wall, it's supposed to turn around in the air after it hits the wall so the feathers trail behind it as it bounces back to you. Let's see if that's true.** Ask:

- **How many times do you think we'll need to bounce it on the wall to prove that it'll always turn around in the air?** (Twice; five times; once for everyone in the classroom.)

Have children line up about 10 feet away from a classroom wall. Show them how to hold the *feather ball* so the feathers are pointing away from the wall. Have each child hold the gizmo by the ball and toss it toward the wall. Every time, the *feather ball* will turn around in the air and return to the child ball-first. Let each child toss it several times.

LEARNING LAB

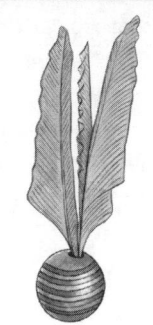

Say: **You did a great job of testing this toy. I guess it really is true—no matter how many times we bounce it on the wall, the** *feather ball* **will always flip around in the air and return to us ball-first. We can count on it. Let's talk about some other things we can count on.** Put the *feather ball* away, then ask:

● **What things can you be sure about?** (That Jesus loves me; that the sun will come up; that Jesus will come again; that I'll be punished if I break the rules.)

Say: **Today we're going to talk about a woman in the Bible who could be counted on. She was dependable, and she was loyal. That means that no matter what happened, people knew that she'd be a good friend. God wants us to be like that, too.** ✦ **God wants us to be loyal to our family and friends.**

 **THE POINT**

RUTH AND NAOMI 📖

(up to 10 minutes)

Say: **Today our story is from the book of Ruth.** Show children the book of Ruth in your Bible. **This story is about three women. The first woman was named Orpah. Whenever I say her name, wave goodbye because she left the other women. Let's practice that: Orpah.** Have children wave good-bye. **The second woman was named Naomi. Whenever I say her name, rub your eyes because she was very sad. Let's practice: Naomi.** Have children rub their eyes. **The third woman was named Ruth. Whenever I say her name, clasp your hands tightly together because she stayed with Naomi. Let's practice: Ruth.** Have children clasp their hands.

Say: **Here's how the story begins. A long time ago, in Israel, there wasn't enough to eat. Some of the people who lived there moved away to find a place where they could grow more food. One of those people was a man named Elimelech (ih-LIM-uh-lek). He took his wife, Naomi, (pause) and his two sons and moved to a place called Moab.**

Soon, Naomi's (pause) husband died, and she was very sad. But she had two sons left. Her sons married women who lived in Moab. One woman was named Orpah (pause). The other was named Ruth (pause). Naomi (pause), Orpah (pause), and Ruth (pause) lived in Moab for 10 years. Then Naomi's (pause) sons died, and the three women were very sad again.

Naomi (pause) decided to go back to Bethlehem where the rest of her family lived. It was hard for women to get by unless they lived with

BIBLE INSIGHT

As a Moabite woman, Ruth could expect to be scorned when she moved to Bethlehem with Naomi. The Moabites had descended from Moab, the son of Lot by an incestuous union with his eldest daughter. This ancestry, plus the seduction of Israelite men by pagan Moabite women, accounted for the disdain felt by the Israelites for the Moabites.

their families. So Naomi (pause), Orpah (pause), and Ruth (pause) packed all their belongings and started on the journey to Bethlehem. Orpah (pause) and Ruth (pause) were willing to leave their homes to live where Naomi's (pause) family lived.

But Naomi (pause) said, "Go back home and live with your mothers. May God be kind to you. I hope God will give you another happy home and new husbands."

Orpah (pause) and Ruth (pause) cried, "No, we want to go with you."

Naomi (pause) said again, "You should go back to your own homes and families. I can't take care of you. You will be much happier there than with me. My life is too sad for you to share."

So Orpah (pause) decided to go back. She kissed Naomi (pause) good-bye and went back home.

Naomi (pause) said to Ruth (pause), "Look, Orpah (pause) is going back to her own people. You should go back with her."

But Ruth (pause) said, "Please don't ask me to leave you. Wherever you go, I'll go. Wherever you live, I'll live. Your people will be my people, and your God will be my God."

When Naomi (pause) heard this, she stopped arguing with Ruth (pause), and they traveled together to Bethlehem. Naomi (pause) wasn't so sad anymore, either.

So let's draw a smile on our faces to replace Naomi's frown (pause). Ask:

● **Why do you think Naomi was happy when Ruth stayed with her?** (Because she had a friend; because she had someone to help her.)

● **How do you feel when your friends stick with you?** (Happy; like my friends care about me.)

Say: **Ruth didn't have to stay with Naomi. Naomi told Ruth that she could go back and live with her own people instead of traveling to Bethlehem. But Ruth loved Naomi and wanted to help her and stay with her. That's what loyalty is. Ruth helped Naomi even when she didn't have to.** ★ **God wants us to be loyal to our family and friends just the way Ruth was loyal to Naomi.**

KEY VERSE Connection

"Sow for yourselves right-eousness, reap the fruit of unfailing love, and break up your unplowed ground; for it is time to seek the Lord, until he comes and showers righteousness on you" (Hosea 10:12).

This Key Verse ties in beautifully with the story of Ruth. Ruth planted goodness by staying with Naomi and working in the fields. She plowed the new ground of knowledge by traveling to a new and unfamiliar land with Naomi. And she harvested the fruit of loyalty by letting Naomi guide her to a fruitful marriage with Boaz.

THE POINT ★

SPIDER-WEB TAG 📖

(up to 10 minutes)

Before class, use masking tape to create a grid on your classroom floor like the one shown in the margin. Make the grid as large as possible.

Have the children stand on the masking tape lines. Choose a volunteer to be the spider. Say: **We're going to play Spider-Web Tag. In this game, everyone must walk on the masking-tape lines—the spider web. If you get tagged by the spider, you must leave the game. If the spider is getting close to one of your classmates, you can reach out, grab your class-**

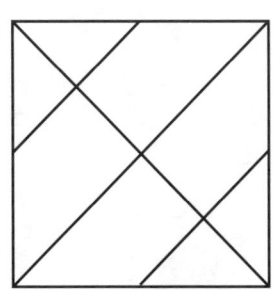

mate by the hand, and gently pull him or her onto your strand of the web. As long as you're holding hands, you're safe, but you can't hold hands for more than five seconds. Ready? Here we go!

Start the game and play for several minutes or until everyone has been tagged. After the game, ask:

● **What did you think when the spider got closer and closer to you?** (I was scared; I felt like I needed a friend to grab me.)

● **How did you feel when a friend saved you from the spider and held your hand to keep you safe?** (Safe; relieved; good.)

● **How did you feel when you kept a friend from being tagged by the spider?** (Like I'd done something really good; like I'd helped out.)

● **What is it like in real life when a friend gives you a helping hand?** (It feels good; it makes me feel loved.)

● **What would have happened if all of you had tried to save yourselves and nobody had grabbed anyone's hand?** (We would've gotten caught sooner; we wouldn't have been loyal to each other.)

Say: **In this game, all of you worked hard to save each other. That's what loyalty is like. Loyalty means that we're always ready to give our friends and our family a helping hand. It means that we try to help them without worrying about what happens to us. Listen to what the Bible says about lending a helping hand to others.** Read **Galatians 6:10** aloud. ✦ **God wants us to be loyal to our family and friends.** Ask:

● **What can you do to be loyal to a friend or someone in your family?** (I can help my little sister when her friends tease her; I can stick up for my friends; I can do nice things for my parents.)

Say: **God is pleased when we're loyal. But it isn't always easy to be loyal. Let's talk more about how we can be loyal to our family and friends.**

Teacher Tip

It's important to say The Point just as it's written in each activity. Repeating The Point over and over will help children remember it and apply it to their lives.

TRUE-BLUE FRIENDS 📖

(up to 15 minutes)

Form groups of three. Say: **I'm going to read aloud some situations. After each one, discuss with your group members what a true-blue friend would do in that situation. To help you know what a true-blue friend is, I'll read you a passage from the Bible.** Read **John 15:9, 12** aloud. **A true-blue friend loves people the way Jesus loves people.**

Read each of the following situations. After each one, give groups time to decide what a true-blue friend would do. Then have volunteers share their groups' ideas with the rest of the class.

SITUATION 1—**James and Brad were walking home from school one day. Brad said, "I'm going to float my new boat in the creek this afternoon. I'm not supposed to play by the creek, so I'm going** to say that I was playing at your house. If my mom asks you, just tell her I spent the whole afternoon at your house." What would a true-blue friend do?

SITUATION 2—Troy was eating cookies and milk and was watching his favorite after-school program on TV. From where he sat, he watched as his dad pulled up to the driveway, stopped the car, got out, and moved two bicycles, a skateboard, a basketball, two jump-ropes, a baseball bat, a ball, a catcher's glove, and a pair of roller skates from the driveway so he could drive his car into the garage. What would a true-blue friend do?

SITUATION 3—From where Sam was sitting, he could see every word on Ted's spelling test. Sam had just learned in Sunday school that cheating makes Jesus sad. Sam knew he shouldn't peek, but spelling was his hardest subject, and his parents had promised him a trip to the ice-cream store if he improved his grades. What would a true-blue friend do?

After you've talked about each of the situations, say: **You had great ideas about what a loyal friend would do. Loyal friends are always ready to help their family and friends. But it's also important that we're loyal to God. We should never help a friend do something that's wrong. That's not being loyal.** ★ **God wants us to be loyal to our family and friends. That means helping our friends do good, godly things. Now let's promise to act like true-blue friends.**

THE POINT ★

Before class, photocopy and cut apart the "True-Blue" handout (p. 26). You'll need one section for each child. Have children write their names on their handout sections. Sprinkle blue powdered drink-mix or gelatin into a shallow bowl. Pour water into another shallow bowl. Have children wet the tips of their fingers in the bowl of water, dip in the bowl of powdered drink-mix, and put blue fingerprints on their handouts. Provide paper towels for clean up. Encourage children to take their handouts home to remind them to be true-blue friends.

We believe that Christian education extends beyond the classroom into the home. **GROWING TOGETHER** Photocopy the "Growing Together" handout (p. 27) for this week, and send it home with your children. Encourage children and parents to use the handout to plan meaningful activities on this week's topic. Follow up the "Growing Together" activities next week by asking children what their families did together.

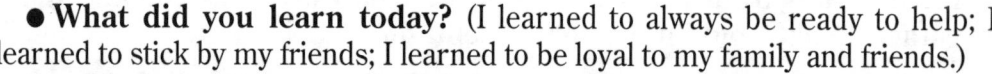 CLOSING

STICK TOGETHER 📖

(up to 10 minutes)

★ THE POINT

Ask:

● **What did you learn today?** (I learned to always be ready to help; I learned to stick by my friends; I learned to be loyal to my family and friends.)

Say: ✦ **God wants us to be loyal to our family, to our friends, and to him. Another way to say that we'll be loyal to people is to say that we'll stick with them through thick and thin. When people stick together, they hold fast to each other.**

Read **Joshua 23:8**: "But you are to hold fast to the Lord your God, as you have until now."

Say: **Let's stick together right now.**

Give each child a *Wikki Stix.* If you have more children than *Wikki Stix,* cut the *Wikki Stix* in half. Have the children press their *Wikki Stix* together to form a sculpture blob. Pass the sculpture around, and have each child shake it to see how well it sticks together.

Say: **When we all stick together, we're very strong, just like this sculpture. Nothing can hurt us or separate us because loyalty is a strong bond that keeps us together. People who are loyal to each other help each other. Let's stick our *Wikki-Stix* sculpture to the door. Then when your parents or brothers or sisters come to pick you up, you can explain that the sculpture reminds us that people who are loyal stick together.**

Have the class help press the *Wikki-Stix* sculpture onto the door. Then close in prayer, asking God to help your children be loyal to him and to others.

IN THE FIELDS NAME TAGS

Photocopy this page and cut the name tags where indicated.
Have the children decorate them and write their names in the blanks.

FAITHFUL AND LOYAL **25**

TRUE-BLUE

Photocopy and cut apart this handout for use during the "True-Blue Friends" activity.

I promise to be

loyal to my family,
loyal to my friends,
and loyal to my God.

I promise to be

loyal to my family,
loyal to my friends,
and loyal to my God.

I promise to be

loyal to my family,
loyal to my friends,
and loyal to my God.

RUTH 1:

God wants us to be loyal to our family and friends.

KEY VERSE

"Sow for yourselves right-eousness, reap the fruit of unfailing love, and break up your unplowed ground; for it is time to seek the Lord, until he comes and showers righteousness on you" (Hosea 10:12).

GROWING TOGETHER

I·N T·O·U·C·H

Today your child learned that loyalty is important. The children practiced being loyal to each other. They learned that being loyal means being ready to lend a helping hand. The children also learned that God is happy when they stick by their family members and friends.

SWEET LOYALTY

Thaw a loaf of frozen bread dough, and separate it into balls the size of your child's fist. Pull each dough ball into a thin circle. Wrap each dough circle around a marshmallow and pinch the dough together to seal the seams. Place the dough balls in a greased 9×13 pan. Put the pan in a warm place, and let the dough rise until doubled. Brush the dough with melted butter, and sprinkle with cinnamon and sugar. Bake according to package directions until golden. Bite into the sweet treats, and talk about the sweet goodness we have inside when we're loyal to family, friends, and God.

TRUE-BLUE

Talk with your child about what it means to be a true-blue friend. Then bake a batch of blueberry muffins with your child. Put the muffins in a basket lined with blue napkins or tissue paper. Design a card on blue paper that says, "We're your true-blue friends." Deliver the gift to a friend or family member.

BALLOON BAG

Use a funnel to pour a cup of small pebbles or sand into a small round balloon. Blow up the balloon and tie it shut. Draw a friendly face on the outside. Put the balloon on a table top. Tap it gently, and it'll bounce back. (Be careful not to tap too hard or the sand will shift and the balloon will be stuck on its side.) Talk about how being loyal and faithful means that no matter what happens with our friends and family, we can always bounce back and be true friends to them.

ME AND MY SHADOW

Read Ephesians 5:1, then turn off all but one light. Direct its light onto a wall. Take turns standing in front of the light so your shadow is cast on the wall. Have fun watching your shadows move. You might want to act out a Bible story or make shadow pictures with your hands. Do joyful motions to praise music. Try to imitate each other's shadows. Then talk about how part of being loyal to God is imitating his character and holiness. Think of ways you can be loyal imitators of God.

W·H·A·T'S M·I·N·E I·S . . .

THE POINT
God wants us to be generous.

THE BIBLE BASIS:
Ruth 2:1-23. Ruth gleans in Boaz's field.

In a perfect world, the rich would be generous with their money, and the poor would be generous with their time. The educated would freely share their knowledge, and laborers would cheerfully provide their skills. Those who could organize people would do so without oppressing them, and those who could heal and comfort would alleviate human suffering.

Even though we don't live in a perfect world, we're still called to be generous with all we have. Teach your children how to do that by showing them the examples set by Ruth and Boaz in the second chapter of Ruth. Ruth and Boaz saw their generosity as nothing more than kindness. But God blessed these two faithful people with a family whose offspring would eventually include King David and God's own Son, Jesus Christ. You can help the children in your class develop a spirit of generosity so that God can use their acts of kindness for his perfect purposes.

Other Scriptures used in this lesson are **Psalm 24:1; 1 Peter 4:10;** and **1 John 3:18, 23.**

KEY VERSE
for Lessons 1–4

"Sow for yourselves righteousness, reap the fruit of unfailing love, and break up your unplowed ground; for it is time to seek the Lord, until he comes and showers righteousness on you" (Hosea 10:12).

GETTING THE POINT

Children will

- learn that everything they have belongs to God;
- discover that they can be generous with their time, their gifts, their affection, and their possessions; and
- learn that each generous act is a precious gift.

Before the lesson, collect the items from the Learning Lab for the activities you plan to use. Refer to the pictures in the margin to see what each item looks like.

THIS LESSON AT A GLANCE

SECTION	MINUTES	WHAT CHILDREN WILL DO	LEARNING LAB SUPPLIES	CLASSROOM SUPPLIES
WELCOME TIME	up to 5	**Welcome!**—Receive a warm welcome from the teacher and make name tags.		"In the Fields Name Tags" (p. 25), scissors, markers, tape or safety pins
ATTENTION GRABBER	up to 10	**Monkey Scramble**—Collect as many monkeys as they can in 30 seconds and find out that it's better to give to others generously than to scramble for things.	Plastic monkeys	
BIBLE EXPLORATION & APPLICATION	up to 10 📖	**Generous Heroes**—Hear the story of Ruth, Naomi, and Boaz from Ruth 2:1-23 and learn that being generous is giving a precious gift.	Wikki Stix, glitter pins	Bible, index cards, marker
	up to 15 📖	**Mosaics**—Learn from 1 John 3:18, 23 that generosity is a way to show love for others, and create gifts to give away.	Cassette: "This Is My Command-ment," "Lyrics Poster"	Bible, cassette player, colored paper, scissors, glue, pencils
	up to 10 📖	**My Gifts**—Listen to 1 Peter 4:10, learn that God has given them many gifts, and play a rhythm game to list all of the things they can give generously.		Bible
CLOSING	up to 10 📖	**It Belongs to God**—Find out from Psalm 24:1 that they can be generous because everything they have belongs to God.	Paper globe	Bible

Remember to make photocopies of the "Growing Together" handout (p. 38) to send home with your children. "Growing Together" is a valuable tool for helping first- and second-graders talk with their parents about what they're learning in class.

ELCOME TIME

WELCOME!
(up to 5 minutes)

● Greet each child individually with an enthusiastic smile.

● Thank each child for coming to class today.

● As children arrive, ask them about last week's "Growing Together" discussion. Use questions such as "How did imitating shadows remind you to imitate God?" and "Who were you a true-blue friend to last week? What did you do?"

● Say: **Today we're going to learn that**  **God wants us to be generous.**

THE POINT ★

● Hand out the name tags children made during Lesson 1, and help them attach the name tags to their clothing. If some of the name tags were damaged, or if children weren't in class that week, have them make new name tags using the photocopiable handout on page 25.

● Tell the children that the attention-getting signal you'll use during this lesson is clapping your hands three times. Ask children to respond by clapping their hands three times and focusing their attention on you. Rehearse the signal with the children, telling them to respond quickly so you have plenty of time for all the fun activities planned for this lesson.

TTENTION GRABBER

MONKEY SCRAMBLE
(up to 10 minutes)

Have children sit on the floor in a circle. Put the *plastic monkeys* in a pile in the middle of the circle. If you have more than seven children, form two groups and give each group half of the monkeys.

LEARNING LAB

Say: **I'll choose a volunteer to start this game. That person will have 30 seconds to hook together as many *plastic monkeys* as possible. To hook the monkeys, pick up one monkey by its body and use its tail to scoop up the other monkeys. You can use only one hand. After 30 seconds, I'll call time by blowing the *balloon squawker,* and you can count**

"Sow for yourselves righteousness, reap the fruit of unfailing love, and break up your unplowed ground; for it is time to seek the Lord, until he comes and showers righteousness on you" (Hosea 10:12).

The generosity of Ruth and Boaz sprang from goodness and loyalty to family. First- and second-graders are beginning to make friends outside the family, but family still comes first. Use the Key Verse to show children that, like Ruth and Boaz, they can be generous and loyal in their own families.

Teacher Tip

It's important to say The Point just as it's written in each activity. Repeating The Point over and over will help children remember it and apply it to their lives.

★ THE POINT

your monkeys. Then you'll give a monkey to the next person in the circle and return the rest of the monkeys to the pile, and we'll start again.

Choose a volunteer to begin the game. Start the game by saying "go." After 30 seconds, call time by blowing into the *balloon squawker* and letting the air squawk out. Have the child count the monkeys that he or she has scooped up by the tail. Continue until every child has had a turn. Determine who scooped up the most monkeys. Congratulate all the children for their hard work. Clap three times to get the children's attention, and wait for them to respond. Ask:

● **What was hard about this game?** (Every time I scooped up a monkey I dropped some; I needed more time to get them all; it was hard not to be able to use both hands.)

Say: **In this game, only one person could play at a time, and that person got to use all the toys.** Ask:

● **Have you ever played with someone in real life who kept all the toys and wouldn't let you use them? What is that like?** (Yes, it's no fun when people won't share; yes, I don't like playing with people who won't share, because I never get a turn.)

Say: **This game was fun. Whoever was playing tried to grab more and more of the toys. But in real life, we're not supposed to grab all the toys. Sometimes people try really hard to grab all the stuff they can, just as all of us tried hard to scoop up all the monkeys. And sometimes, when people get a lot of stuff, they don't like to share it with others. We call that being selfish. Today we're going to talk about being generous, which is the opposite of being selfish. Let's play a game about being generous.**

Give each child a *plastic monkey.* Say: **In this game, you'll give your *plastic monkey* to someone else. As you give your monkey away, someone may give you a monkey. Give it away as soon as you can. You can never have more than one monkey at a time, and you can't give a monkey to the same person who gave one to you.**

Play the game for a minute or two. Then call time by blowing into the *balloon squawker* and letting the air squawk out. Put the *plastic monkeys* away, and gather the children on the floor. Ask:

● **Which game was more fun? Explain.** (The first game, because it was harder; the second game, because we all played; the second game, because I got to play the whole time.)

Say: ★ **God wants us to be generous with what we have. In the second game, all of you were generous, and you had fun the whole time. When we're generous, we make others happy, and we have fun ourselves. Our Bible story today is about people who were generous with everything they had. Let's find out what happened.**

BIBLE EXPLORATION & APPLICATION

GENEROUS HEROES 📖

(up to 10 minutes)

Bend the *Wikki Stix* into five stick-people—Ruth, Naomi, Boaz, and two harvesters. Use index cards to make name tags for them. Gather the children by a classroom wall. Stick the figures to the wall so they're at eye level when you're sitting on the floor. Put the *glitter pins* on the floor beneath the figures.

Point to each figure as you say its name. Say: **Today's story is about Ruth, Naomi, a man named Boaz, and two harvesters who worked in Boaz's field. The story comes from the book of Ruth.** Show children the book of Ruth in your Bible. Keep the Bible open to **Ruth 2:1-23** as you tell the story.

Say: **While I tell the story, listen for times the characters were generous with each other. That could mean they were generous with time, money, compliments, or anything. Being generous means sharing whatever you have with the people around you. I'll pause each time there's a generous act, and you can take turns putting a** *glitter pin* **jewel on the figure who was generous. Let's begin.**

One day, Ruth said to Naomi, "We need some food. I'm going to the fields. Maybe someone will be kind enough to let me gather the leftover grain that falls behind as it's harvested." Ruth had come to Bethlehem with Naomi to help take care of her. Pause.

Naomi knew they needed food to eat, so she said, "Go to the fields, my daughter, and see what you can gather for us."

Ruth walked to the fields. The workers were cutting the grain and gathering it in small bundles. They worked hard. Some of the grain fell out of the bundles, and the workers left it in the fields for poor people to gather and take home to eat. Pause. Ruth walked behind the workers and gathered the grain the workers left behind. Pause.

The field where Ruth was gathering grain belonged to a man named Boaz. Boaz was related to Naomi's husband, who had died in Moab. Soon Boaz came to visit his field to see how the work was going. Boaz could see that his workers were working very hard, so he called out to them, "May God be with you!" Pause.

The workers called back to him, "May God bless you!" Pause.

Boaz watched Ruth working hard to gather grain to feed Naomi and herself. Boaz asked the servant who was in charge of the workers, "Who is that girl gleaning grain?"

The servant answered, "She is the young woman from Moab who came back with Naomi. She said, 'Please let me follow the workers and gather the grain that they leave behind.' She came in the morning and

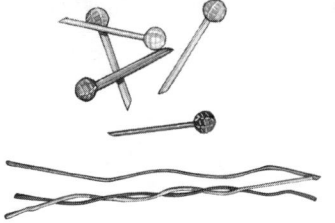
BIBLE INSIGHT

Boaz made sure his workers followed Mosaic law, which required reapers to leave crops in certain areas of the fields so that the poor and travelers might follow behind them and gather that grain. Harvest time began in mid-April and was characterized by intense heat, so Boaz's extra kindness to Ruth must have been welcome.

has been working ever since. Pause. She stopped for only a few moments to rest in the shelter."

Boaz called out to Ruth and said, "Listen, Ruth. Don't go to gather grain for yourself in another field. Don't leave this field at all, but follow closely behind the workers in my field. I have warned everyone not to bother you. When you're thirsty, go and drink from the water jugs that the young men have filled." Pause.

Ruth said, "I'm a stranger in your country. Why have you been so kind to me?"

Boaz said, "I know how you've helped your mother-in-law. You left your mother and father and your own country to come to a nation where you didn't know anyone. May God reward you." Pause.

Ruth said, "I want to continue to please you, sir. You've said kind and encouraging words to me even though I'm not one of your servants." Pause.

At mealtime, Boaz invited Ruth to share his lunch, (pause) so Ruth sat down and ate lunch with him. Boaz gave her bread to eat and invited her to dip it in his sauce. He also gave her roasted grain to eat. Ruth ate until she was full, and she had food left over.

When Ruth went back to work, Boaz called his workers aside and told them to let Ruth gather grain from anywhere in the field, even from the piles that the workers had gathered. Boaz even told his workers to drop some of the best grain for Ruth to gather. Pause.

Ruth worked hard all day long. When it came time to stop in the evening, she separated the good kernels of grain from the outside skins. Ruth had gathered a lot of grain because Boaz had been so kind to her. Pause.

When Ruth got home, she gave the grain to Naomi. She also gave Naomi the leftovers from her lunch. Pause. Naomi was very pleased when she saw how much food Ruth had gathered. She said, "Ruth, tell me whose field you worked in today. May God bless whoever noticed you!"

Ruth told Naomi that she'd worked in Boaz's field.

Naomi praised God when she heard the news. Pause. She said, "Boaz continues to be kind to us. He's one of our close relatives—a relative who should take care of us."

Ruth told Naomi about all of the kind, generous things Boaz had done for her. Naomi told Ruth to continue working in Boaz's field. Ruth did as Naomi asked. Pause. She worked until the barley was harvested and until the wheat was harvested, and she continued to live with Naomi.

Say: When we do kind deeds because we want to, we're being generous. Each time we're generous, it's like giving a precious gift. Ruth, Naomi, and Boaz were generous to each other. Look at all the precious gifts they gave each other. Have children count the *glitter pins*.

Say: In this story, we counted 15 precious gifts of generosity. God gave to the people generously, too. **Let's use the rest of the *glitter pins* to count some of the generous things God gave to them.** Have children count out *glitter pins* to represent God's gifts. They might think of ideas such as God's gifts of sunshine and rain to make the grain grow or God's gifts of love and protection.

Say: **Look at all these precious gifts of generosity. Ruth, Naomi, and Boaz were generous to each other, and God was generous to them.** ✦ **God wants us to be generous, too. Let's find out why.**

Return the *Wikki-Stix* figures and the *glitter pins* to the Learning Lab. You'll need two of the figures for the next lesson, "Listen Up."

THE POINT ★

MOSAICS 📖

(up to 15 minutes)

Before class, cut different-colored paper into ¼-inch squares. Here's an easy way to do it: Cut the paper into long strips ¼-inch wide. This will go quickly if you use a paper cutter. Stack the strips and snip them into tiny squares. Keep the colors separate.

Cue the *cassette tape* to "This Is My Commandment." During class, set out the paper squares, half sheets of colored paper, pencils, and glue.

Say: **Listen to what the Bible says about being generous.** Read **1 John 3:18, 23** aloud. **God wants us to love each other. It's God's commandment to us. Let's sing a song about loving each other.** Sing "This Is My Commandment" with the *cassette tape.* Choose a volunteer to hold the "Lyrics Poster." Choose another volunteer to point to the words as you sing them.

After the song, turn off the cassette player, put the "Lyrics Poster" away, and say: **One way we can make our joy full is to give generously to people we love. Let's each make a picture to give to a friend or family member. Choose a sheet of paper. Then lightly draw a picture with a pencil. Then fill in the shapes by gluing these tiny paper squares to the picture. Be generous as you make the picture by using lots of tiny paper squares.**

While children are creating their mosaics, talk about generosity. Ask:

● **When have people been generous to you? Tell me what they did that was generous.** (My mom is generous when she bakes cookies for me; my brother is generous when he lets me play with his basketball.)

● **What was it like when these people were generous to you?** (Good; I felt like they trusted me; I felt like my mom loves me.)

● **Have you ever been generous with someone? What did you do?** (I gave a special gift to my dad; I gave my stuffed animals away to kids who don't have any.)

● **How did you feel when you were generous?** (Special; like I helped someone.)

● **Why do you think it's important to be generous with others?** (Because God wants us to be generous; because it's nice; because it keeps us from being selfish.)

LEARNING LAB

Teacher Tip
This project will go faster using half sheets of paper as the background for the mosaics because there will be less room to fill with paper squares.

Teacher Tip
Picture-making will be easier if you squirt some glue on a piece of paper. Have children dip the tips of their index fingers in the glue and use their sticky fingers to pick up the paper squares.

When the children have finished their pictures, set the artwork aside to dry. As you set each picture aside, have the artist say who he or she will give the picture to.

THE POINT

Say: **I'm proud of each of you! You put a generous amount of hard work into making these pictures to show your love for someone else.** ✦ **God wants us to be generous. I know God is pleased with each of you right now.**

Have children help put the art supplies away.

MY GIFTS

(up to 10 minutes)

Have children sit cross-legged in a circle so their knees touch their neighbors' knees. Say: **I'll read a Bible verse. Listen for the generous gift that God has given you.** Read **1 Peter 4:10.** Say: **God has given us many things that we can be generous with. Any time we're helpful or we give time or money to others, we're being generous. We're going to play a game to help us think of ways to be generous. To help us get started, let's think about our Bible story.** Ask:

● **What did Ruth, Boaz, Naomi, and the harvesters do that was generous?** (Boaz let Ruth gather food; the harvesters dropped extra grain; Ruth took care of Naomi.)

● **What can you do to be generous?** (I can spend time with my grandmother; I can give some of my allowance to the church; I can teach my brother how to play Checkers.)

Say: **Super ideas! Now let's use your great ideas in this game.** Teach the children this saying:

Generous gifts God gives to me.
Generous gifts I'll give to you.
I'll be generous with my _____.

Have the children think of one-word answers to go in the blank, such as time, money, love, or games. Then teach them this clapping rhythm.

● Slap your thighs twice.
● Cross your hands and slap your knees twice.
● Uncross your hands and slap your knees twice.
● Reach out and slap your neighbors' knees twice.

Put the saying and the clapping rhythm together so that children slap their neighbors' knees as they end the saying. Go around the circle, and have each child complete the sentence as you repeat the saying and clap the rhythm.

When each child has completed the sentence at least once, say: **There are so many ways to be generous with each other that we can be generous every day.** ✦ **God wants us to be generous with whatever we have every day.**

THE POINT

CLOSING

IT BELONGS TO GOD 📖

(up to 10 minutes)

Ask:
● **What did you learn today?** (I learned that I should give things to other people; I learned that I should share; I learned that God wants me to be generous.)

Take the *paper globe* out of its wrapper, and show it to the children. Say: **Right now this world is empty. But we're going to fill it with everything that we have. Tell me about some of the things that you have that you can give to or share with others.** Have the children call out answers, such as bicycles, basketballs, clothes, food, and time. For each answer they call out, puff a small amount of air into the *paper globe* to blow it up.

Say: **Listen to what God's Word says about all of these things of the earth.** Read **Psalm 24:1** aloud. **Everything we have and everything we see belongs to God. God wants us to be wise and careful with the things that we've been given.**

Allow the children to gently bat the globe around the room without letting it hit the floor. Make sure each child gets a chance to bat the globe. Remind children that the *paper globe* is fragile and will break if they hit it too hard.

Put the globe away, then say: **Thank you for treating the paper globe so gently. I know that you'll be just as careful with the real gifts that God gives. Being wise and careful with the gifts God gives us means always being ready to share them with others.** ✦ **God wants us to be generous. To show that we want to be generous with what we have, let's generously give our handshakes to each other.** Take a minute to let children shake hands with each other.

Then close the class with prayer, thanking God for his generous gifts and asking for help to share his gifts generously with others.

THE POINT

RUTH 2:
God wants us to be generous.

KEY VERSE

"Sow for yourselves righteousness, reap the fruit of unfailing love, and break up your unplowed ground; for it is time to seek the Lord, until he comes and showers righteousness on you" (Hosea 10:12).

GROWING TOGETHER

I·N T·O·U·C·H

Today your child learned that he or she has been given gifts and possessions that can be shared with others. The children learned that being generous is like giving precious gifts of love to others and that generosity is pleasing to God. Use these activities to encourage your child to be generous every day.

GIFT BASKETS
• • • • • • • • • •

Put together a gift basket of fun and useful items for a grandparent or an elderly church member. Have your child help think of items to include. You might want to put in magazines, a book of crossword puzzles, a pretty handkerchief, bath soaps, hand lotion, homemade cookies, bread, jam, or homemade artwork. Create a cheerful card, and deliver the basket with your child.

MONEY MATTERS
• • • • • • • • • •

Encourage your child to try this method of dividing allowance and birthday money. Set out three jars. Label the jars "spending," "savings," and "church and charity." Help your child decide how to divide the money among the three jars. Encourage your child to wisely spend the money from the spending jar. Once a month visit the bank together, and deposit the savings-jar money. Then count the money in the church-and-charity jar, and discuss how much to give to your church and how much to give to charity. Suggest charities such as the Red Cross, a toys-for-tots program, a local soup kitchen, or your denomination's missionary program. If possible, have your child personally give the money to the charity.

NEIGHBORLY GENEROSITY
• • • • • • • • • •

Practice generosity with neighbors or church friends. Invite several families over for a potluck at your home one evening this week. Have your child help choose and prepare a main dish, a beverage, and a dessert to serve. Ask your guests to bring salads, vegetables, bread, and fruit dishes to round out the meal. Afterward, talk about how each family member shared generously so that everyone could enjoy a special meal.

GLEANINGS
• • • • • • • • • •

Visit a nature area or park near your home. "Glean" fallen natural objects such as pine cones, twigs, and leaves. Don't pick any living plants. When you get home, spray the items with a generous amount of hair spray. Then arrange them in a basket or vase, and put the bouquet on your table. Before each meal, look at the basket, and thank God for providing everything you need—even beautiful decorations.

L·I·S·T·E·N

U·P

⭐ ## THE POINT
Good advice can
help us follow God.

THE BIBLE BASIS: 📖

Ruth 3:1-15. Ruth follows Naomi's plan.

Ruth needed good advice. She was a stranger in a new country where she found unusual customs and unfamiliar beliefs. Ruth wanted to do the right thing. She earnestly desired to follow God, but she needed good advice to keep from making mistakes. Naomi was able to offer Ruth good advice because Naomi's wisdom came from God. Ruth was fortunate to have a loyal friend like Naomi. And Ruth wisely heeded the advice Naomi offered.

People who can count on friends and family for trustworthy advice are fortunate. But the best advice in the world is available to anyone who takes the time to look in God's Word. The psalmist said, "Your statutes are my delight; they are my counselors" (Psalm 119:24). You can teach your students that the best advice, the kind that can help them follow God, comes from God's own Word and from the people who serve God.

Other Scriptures used in this lesson are **Proverbs 16:24; 19:20; Hebrews 10:24;** and **2 Timothy 2:22.**

KEY VERSE
for Lessons 1–4

"Sow for yourselves righteousness, reap the fruit of unfailing love, and break up your unplowed ground; for it is time to seek the Lord, until he comes and showers righteousness on you" (Hosea 10:12).

GETTING THE POINT

Children will

- practice choosing whose advice to listen to,
- find out where to go for advice to help them follow God, and
- give good advice to one another.

Before the lesson, collect the items from the Learning Lab for the activities you plan to use. Refer to the pictures in the margin to see what each item looks like.

THIS LESSON AT A GLANCE

SECTION	MINUTES	WHAT CHILDREN WILL DO	LEARNING LAB SUPPLIES	CLASSROOM SUPPLIES
WELCOME TIME	up to 5	**Welcome!**—Receive a warm welcome from the teacher and make name tags.		"In the Fields Name Tags" (p. 25), scissors, markers, tape or safety pins
ATTENTION GRABBER	up to 10	**Who to Listen To**—Listen to advice from classmates and decide who is telling the truth.	Feather ball	
BIBLE EXPLORATION & APPLICATION	up to 10	**Naomi's Advice**—Listen to the story of Ruth and Naomi from Ruth 3:1-15 and talk about deciding whether the advice they get is good.	Cassette: "Naomi's Advice"	Bible, cassette player
	up to 15	**Good and Bad**—Talk about needing good advice, then play a game based on Hebrews 10:24 and 2 Timothy 2:22 to practice what to do when they get good or bad advice.	Wikki-Stix figures, foam person, glitter pins, felt strips, plastic rings	Bible
	up to 15	**Advice to Wear**—Make paper hats, listen to Proverbs 16:24 and 19:20, and write their own proverbs to help others follow God.		Bible, paper, tape, markers
CLOSING	up to 5	**Advice Song**—Sing a song that tells where to go for good advice and ask God's help in listening to advice.	"Lyrics Poster"	

Remember to make photocopies of the "Growing Together" handout (p. 47) to send home with your children. "Growing Together" is a valuable tool for helping first- and second-graders talk with their parents about what they're learning in class.

WELCOME TIME

WELCOME!
(up to 5 minutes)

- Greet each child individually with an enthusiastic smile.
- Thank each child for coming to class today.
- As children arrive, ask them about last week's "Growing Together" discussion. Use questions such as "Which of God's gifts did you notice last week?" and "How were you generous last week?"
- Say: **Today we're going to learn that ⭐ good advice can help us follow God.**
- Hand out the name tags children made during Lesson 1, and help them attach the name tags to their clothing. If some of the name tags were damaged, or if children weren't in class that week, have them make new name tags using the photocopiable handout on page 25.
- Tell the children that the attention-getting signal you'll use during this lesson is clapping your hands three times. Ask children to respond by clapping their hands three times and focusing their attention on you. Rehearse the signal with the children, telling them to respond quickly so you have plenty of time for all the fun activities planned for this lesson.

THE POINT

ATTENTION GRABBER

WHO TO LISTEN TO
(up to 10 minutes)

LEARNING LAB

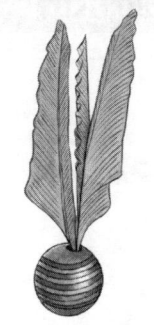

Choose one volunteer to be the "finder." Have the finder step outside the room. Choose another volunteer to be the "hider." Say: **The hider is going to hide the _feather ball,_ which we'll call the "treasure." When the finder comes back into the room, the hider will tell the truth about where the treasure is hidden. For example, the hider might say, "Listen to my advice. The treasure is hidden under the table." Everyone else will try to fool the finder by saying the treasure is somewhere else. For example, someone might say,**

KEY VERSE
Connection

"Sow for yourselves right-eousness, reap the fruit of unfailing love, and break up your unplowed ground; for it is time to seek the Lord, until he comes and show-ers righteousness on you" (Hosea 10:12).

Ruth followed Naomi's good advice and was blessed with a husband, son, and happy home. Children need to learn that if they follow the good advice of the Bible, good-ness will follow, just as this Key Verse promises.

★ THE POINT

"Listen to my advice. The treasure is hidden on top of the piano," or "Listen to my advice. The treasure is hidden in the desk drawer."

Have the hider hide the treasure. Bring the finder back into the room, and say: **You may ask as many people as you want to find out where we've hidden the treasure. Then you have to choose whose advice to follow. You can only look in one place, so be careful about who you choose to listen to.**

Have the finder ask several children where the treasure is and then look in the one place he or she thinks the treasure is hidden. Give the finder a round of applause for finding the treasure or for a good try if he or she didn't find the treasure. If the finder is unsuccessful, have the hider show where the treasure was hidden.

Choose another finder and another hider, and play the game again. Play sev-eral rounds of the game as time allows.

After the game, gather the children and ask:

● **How did you decide who to listen to in this game?** (I picked my friend; I picked Sarah because she always tells the truth.)

● **What did you think when you chose correctly? when you chose in-correctly?** (I thought I was lucky; I was surprised that I didn't pick right; I was disappointed.)

● **Do you ever have trouble deciding who's giving you good advice in real life? What do you do?** (I decide for myself what to do; I believe my friends; I ask my dad what to do.)

Say: **Today we're going to talk about advice because ★ good advice can help us follow God. The person in our Bible story today needed good advice, but the advice she got sounded kind of strange. We're go-ing to find out what she did.**

 BIBLE EXPLORATION & APPLICATION

NAOMI'S ADVICE 📖

(up to 10 minutes)

LEARNING LAB

Cue the tape to "Naomi's Advice." Say: **Our story on this *cassette tape* comes from Ruth 3:1-15.** Show children the story in your Bible. **Listen for the advice Ruth was given in this story.** Have children sit in a circle to lis-ten to the story. When the story ends, turn off the cassette player, and ask:

● **If I told you to lift the blankets off someone's bed and curl up by their feet, would you think that was good advice? Why or why not?** (Yes, if I knew I could trust you; no, it sounds silly to me.)

● **Why do you think Ruth followed the advice that Naomi gave her?** (Because Naomi was her good friend; because she trusted Naomi; because she knew she was supposed to do what she was told.)

● **Whose advice do you follow? Why?** (My mom's, because I'm supposed to obey her; the minister's, because he knows a lot about God; my big sister's, because she'd hit me if I didn't.)

● **Whose advice don't you follow? Why?** (My next door neighbor's, because he's always getting in trouble; my cousin's, because she doesn't believe in Jesus.)

Say: **There are lots of people who give us advice, but not all advice is good advice. We need to listen to people we trust so we can be sure that what they tell us is good advice. Let's find out more about the difference between good advice and bad advice.**

GOOD AND BAD 📖

(up to 15 minutes)

You'll need the *Wikki-Stix* figures you made in Lesson 2. Put one *Wikki-Stix* figure on the *foam person's* right shoulder and another *Wikki-Stix* figure on the *foam person's* left shoulder. Use *glitter pins* to secure the figures to the foam.

Say: **Some cartoons show two characters sitting on someone's shoulders like this. Let's pretend that one figure is someone who always gives good advice, such as "You shouldn't eat that candy before dinner." We'll pretend the other figure is someone who gives bad advice, such as "Go ahead and eat the candy. It'll taste so good, and no one will ever know." I'm going to read aloud some situations. Then we'll think of good advice to give in each situation.**

Form pairs. Read the situations one by one. After each one, have partners think of good advice for that situation. Give them a minute for discussion, then have children share their advice with the rest of the class. As the children share their advice, ask them how their advice would help the characters follow God.

SITUATION 1—**Connie went to the coat room after school to get her lunch box, but it wasn't there. She was very upset because the lunch box was special—it was her favorite color, and it was a gift from her favorite aunt. On the way home from school, Connie saw that Melanie was carrying a lunch box that looked just like the one she lost. What good advice can you give to Connie?**

SITUATION 2—**Bobby was playing at Tommy's house after school. They had a big fight about what game to play next. Tommy finally yelled, "If you want to play that stupid game, then you can just go home." What good advice can you give to Bobby?**

SITUATION 3—**Nate had just moved into a new neighborhood with**

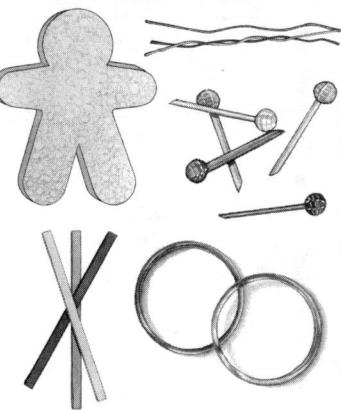
BIBLE INSIGHT

According to Hebrew law, if a man died, his brother was required to marry his widow so their firstborn son could carry on the family name. So Naomi herself had a greater right to claim assistance from Boaz than did Ruth, since Boaz was actually related to Elimelech, Naomi's deceased husband. But Naomi relinquished those claims in favor of her daughter-in-law.

lots of other kids his own age. When Nate went outside to play with the other kids, they said he couldn't play with them unless he threw a rock at Mrs. Carlson's house. Mrs. Carlson was an old woman who lived by herself in their neighborhood. What good advice can you give to Nate?

After pairs have shared their advice, say: **Good ideas! Now let's play a game about giving good advice and about what to do when we get bad advice.**

Prop the *foam person* against the wall. Use six *felt strips* to create an oblong box on the floor on the "good advice" side of the *foam person*. Have children line up several feet away.

Say: **Listen to this verse, and tell me what Christians should do for each other.** Read **Hebrews 10:24.** Ask:

● **What should we do for each other?** (Help each other do good things.)

Say: **Now listen to this verse, and tell me what we should do when we hear about bad things.** Read **2 Timothy 2:22.** Ask:

● **What should we do when we hear about bad things?** (Run away from them; flee.)

Say: **Let's play a game, using what we've learned from these verses. Each of you will have a chance to toss a *plastic ring* into the box on the good-advice side. If the ring lands inside the box, jump up and down, cheer, and clap your hands because the Bible says in Hebrews 10:24 that we should help each other do good. We can do that by cheering for each other, encouraging each other, and giving each other good advice. If the *plastic ring* lands outside the good-advice box, that means it's in the bad-advice territory. Then you will all walk around the room as fast as you can and then get back in line because the good advice given in 2 Timothy 2:22 says that we should run away from evil.**

Play the game, giving each child a chance to toss a *plastic ring* at least once. Put the gizmos away, then get children's attention by clapping three times. Wait for children to respond. Then say:  **Good advice can help us follow God. It's great when we get good advice, but even when we get bad advice there's something good we can do. The Bible tells us to run away from evil. We can always run away from bad advice and look for good advice instead. Now let's make hats that will make good advice easy to find.**

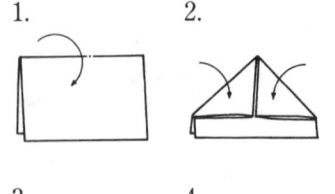 **THE POINT**

ADVICE TO WEAR 📖

(up to 15 minutes)

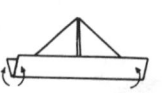

Give each child a sheet of paper. Have the children follow these instructions to create paper hats.

1. Fold the paper in half the short way.
2. From the folded edge, fold the corners over so they meet in the middle.
3. Fold up the flaps at the bottom.

4. Fold the corners of the flaps over and tape.

Have the children write "Good advice can help me follow God" around the edge of the hat.

Say: **Now let's make up proverbs to write on our hats so we can give good advice to anyone who sees our hats. Proverbs are wise sayings of good advice that help us know what will please God. Listen to a proverb from the Bible.** Read this version of **Proverbs 16:24,** or read it from an easy-to-understand version: **"Pleasant words are a honeycomb, sweet to the soul and healing to the bones."**

Have the children come up with their own proverbs to illustrate or write on the hats. They may use these beginnings to get started:

● Godly people always...
● God is pleased when...
● Wise children never...

When the children have written their proverbs on their hats, have them put on their hats. Say: **Listen to what happens when we listen to advice.** Read **Proverbs 19:20** aloud. **All of you look like people who are on their way to being wise.**  **Good advice can help us follow God. And when we follow God, we show that we're wise.**

THE POINT ★

**e believe that Christian education extends beyond the classroom into the home.** Photocopy the "Growing Together" handout (p. 47) for this week, and send it home with your children. Encourage children and parents to use the handout to plan meaningful activities on this week's topic. Follow up the "Growing Together" activities next week by asking children what their families did together.

LEARNING LAB

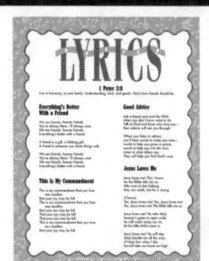

CLOSING

ADVICE SONG

(up to 5 minutes)

Say: **Today we learned that**  **good advice can help us follow God. But we need to know where to look for good advice.** Ask:

● **Where do you look for good advice?** (The Bible; my mom and dad; God; my teachers; my best friend; a policeman.)

THE POINT ★

Say: **Let's sing a song about looking for good advice.**

Sing the song "Good Advice" to the tune of "Hark! The Herald Angels Sing."

Choose a volunteer to hold the "Lyrics Poster." Choose another child to point to the words as you sing. The second time through the song, teach the children the actions.

Good Advice

Lyrics	Actions
Ask a friend, and read the Bible.	(Point to someone, and hold hands open in front of you like a book.)
When you don't know what to do,	(Shrug your shoulders.)
Talk to God and those who love you.	(Fold hands in prayer, and hug yourself.)
Their advice will see you through.	(Open and close your hand to imitate a person talking.)
When you listen to advice,	(Cup your hand by your ear.)
You'll hear words to make you wise,	(Point to your head.)
Words to help you grow in grace,	(Raise your hand above your head to indicate growth.)
Words to help you win the race.	(Pump arms as if you're running.)
Listen to what others say,	(Cup your hand behind your ear.)
They will help you find God's way.	(Shield your eyes with your hand as if you're looking for something.)

After the song, close your class with prayer, asking God to help the children listen to good advice that will help them follow God.

RUTH 3:

Good advice can help us follow God.

KEY VERSE

"Sow for yourselves righteousness, reap the fruit of unfailing love, and break up your unplowed ground; for it is time to seek the Lord, until he comes and showers righteousness on you" (Hosea 10:12).

GROWING TOGETHER

Today children learned that they can get lots of good advice from the Bible and other Christians to help them know, love, and follow God. The children learned where to go to find good advice and what to do when they get bad advice. Use these activities at home to help your child recognize and follow good advice.

WISE-WORD TREATS

Write words of wise biblical advice on strips of paper. Include verses such as Proverbs 3:3; Proverbs 15:1; Proverbs 21:21; Proverbs 24:14; and Proverbs 25:11. Then make Rice Krispies Treats. Instead of putting the cookie mixture in a pan, mold it in a well-buttered kitchen funnel. Wrap the treats in foil and put a strip of advice in each one so that the treats look like giant Hershey's Kisses. Distribute these wise-word treats to friends and family members.

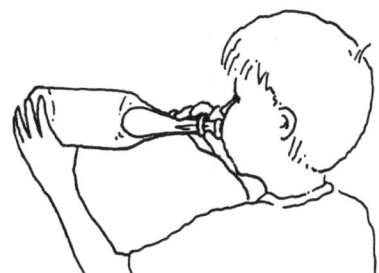

FOOLISH HEARERS

Holding the open end of an uninflated balloon, put the balloon inside a soda pop bottle. Blow into the balloon to try to inflate it. The balloon won't inflate much, no matter how hard you blow. Compare the balloon to a foolish person who is given good advice but refuses to take it. Then take the balloon out of the bottle, and blow it up. Compare that to a wise person who listens to the counsel of many wise people. Talk about who you can listen to to get good advice.

INTERVIEWS

Ask a grandparent or an older church friend over for an afternoon tea. Serve biscuits with honey, tiny pimento cheese or peanut butter sandwiches, and cookies along with the tea. Remind your child of the words in Proverbs 16:24 as you're making the biscuits and honey: "Pleasant words are a honeycomb, sweet to the soul and healing to the bones." Interview your guest about the best words of advice he or she ever heard and ever gave.

REFRIGERATOR COUNSEL

Read Proverbs 6:20 and Proverbs 12:26. Then write your own proverbs. Begin with "A wise parent never _____ because_____" or "A wise child is like _____" or "Wise people remember to _____." Compare your proverbs with your child's proverbs. Write them all on a sheet of paper, and hang them on the refrigerator. Remind each other to listen to the wise advice of the proverbs.

Permission to photocopy this handout from Group's Hands-On Bible Curriculum™ for Grades 1 and 2 granted for local church use. Copyright © Group Publishing, Inc., P.O. Box 481, Loveland, CO 80539.

I P·R·O·M·I·S·E!

THE POINT
God wants us to keep our promises.

THE BIBLE BASIS:

Ruth 4:1-15. Boaz and Ruth are married.

Promises, promises. We hear them all the time, but we don't always believe them. That could be because the average promise is often only half a promise. Adults can usually tell a half-promise from the genuine kind. But when children hear "Buy this toy, and you'll be happy," or "This won't hurt at all," they expect the promise to be kept. When it isn't, children quickly learn that it's OK to make promises without keeping them. Children need to know that a genuine promise starts with words and good intentions, but it isn't complete until the promise is kept.

Some promises can be made and kept in a short time. Boaz promised that he would settle the question of Ruth's status quickly, and he kept that promise the very next day. Other promises are kept little by little, day by day over a lifetime. Ruth spent her life keeping her promise to Naomi that "your people will be my people, and your God will be my God." Whether it takes a short or long time, a promise is not a promise until it's kept. And God wants us to keep our promises.

Other Scriptures used in this lesson are **Ecclesiastes 5:4-5; Proverbs 12:22b;** and **Ephesians 4:25.**

KEY VERSE
for Lessons 1–4

"Sow for yourselves righteousness, reap the fruit of unfailing love, and break up your unplowed ground; for it is time to seek the Lord, until he comes and showers righteousness on you" (Hosea 10:12).

GETTING THE POINT

Children will

- discover the importance of making promises they can keep,
- find out how to stand against the distractions that make it hard to keep promises, and
- learn that when promises are broken, people can be hurt.

Before the lesson, collect the items from the Learning Lab for the activities you plan to use. Refer to the pictures in the margin to see what each item looks like.

THIS LESSON AT A GLANCE

SECTION	MINUTES	WHAT CHILDREN WILL DO	LEARNING LAB SUPPLIES	CLASSROOM SUPPLIES
WELCOME TIME	up to 5	**Welcome!**—Receive a warm welcome from the teacher and make name tags.		"In the Fields Name Tags" (p. 25), scissors, markers, tape or safety pins
ATTENTION GRABBER	up to 10	**Don't Drop the Ball**—Play a game in which they can't let a ball drop and learn that promises should always be kept.	Feather ball	
BIBLE EXPLORATION & APPLICATION	up to 10	**Boaz Marries Ruth**—Act out the story from Ruth 4:1-15 and find out that Ruth and Boaz faithfully kept their promises.		Bible
	up to 10	**Tall Tales**—Write a tall tale and learn that not keeping a promise is like telling a lie or a tall tale, then read in Ephesians 4:25 that God is displeased when we tell lies.		Bible, pen
	up to 15	**Promise Bouquets**—Make bouquets that represent the precious gift of a kept promise and learn from Proverbs 12:22b that God is pleased when people keep their promises.	Flower foam	Bible, scissors, glue or tape, construction paper, markers
CLOSING	up to 10	**Trust Me**—Agree to be the kind of people who can be trusted to keep promises.		Tootsie Pop lollipops

Remember to make photocopies of the "Growing Together" handout (p. 59) to send home with your children. "Growing Together" is a valuable tool for helping first- and second-graders talk with their parents about what they're learning in class.

T·H·E L·E·S·S·O·N

WELCOME TIME

WELCOME!
(up to 5 minutes)

- Greet each child individually with an enthusiastic smile.
- Thank each child for coming to class today.
- As children arrive, ask them about last week's "Growing Together" discussion. Use questions such as "How was the balloon in a bottle like a person who doesn't listen to good advice?" and "What proverbs did you and your family write?"
- Say: **Today we're going to learn that** ✦ **God wants us to keep our promises.**

THE POINT ✦

- Hand out the name tags the children made during Lesson 1, and help them attach the name tags to their clothing. If some of the name tags were damaged, or if children weren't in class that week, have them make new name tags using the photocopiable handout on page 25.
- Tell the children that the attention-getting signal you'll use during this lesson is clapping your hands three times. Ask children to respond by clapping their hands three times and focusing their attention on you. Rehearse the signal with the children, telling them to respond quickly so you have plenty of time for all the fun activities planned for this lesson.

MODULE REVIEW

Use the casual interaction time at the beginning of class to ask children the following module-review questions.

- **How can you be loyal to your family and friends? How can you be loyal to God?**
- **What does it mean to be generous? What can you share with others?**
- **Where can you look for good advice?**
- **How is your life different because of what we've learned in this class during the last few weeks?**

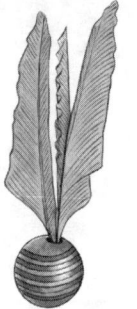**A**TTENTION GRABBER

DON'T DROP THE BALL
(up to 10 minutes)

Gather children around a small table. Have them stand fairly close to each other.

Say: **We used the *feather ball* in another lesson to show what loyalty is. The ball shows loyalty because every time you bounce it against a wall, it flips in the air and comes back to you with the feathers trailing behind.** Demonstrate this for any children who weren't in class during that lesson by throwing the ball at the wall a couple of times.

Say: **Today we're going to talk about keeping promises. Because keeping promises is something that loyal people do, we're going to use the *feather ball* again. In this game, try to blow the *feather ball* off the other side of the table—you can't use your hands at all. Don't let the ball fall off your side of the table, either. Ready? Here we go.**

Put the *feather ball* in the center of the table, and have the children start blowing. When the *feather ball* does fall off the table, start the game again. Play for several minutes, making sure every child participates. After the game, get children's attention by clapping your hands three times. Wait for children to respond. Put the *feather ball* in your lap. Then ask:

● **How did you feel when the ball came close to your edge of the table?** (Scared that it would fall off my side; excited, because it was my turn to keep it away.)

Say: **Sometimes when we're afraid of doing something wrong and letting other people down, we call that being afraid of "dropping the ball."** Ask:

● **Have you ever been afraid of dropping the ball in real life? Tell me about it.** (Yes, once on my baseball team I had to get a hit or my team would lose; yes, once I was in a play, and I was afraid I'd forget my line.)

● **Has anyone ever broken a promise to you? How did that make you feel?** (Yes, my uncle promised he'd visit on my birthday, and I was sad when he couldn't come; I was mad when my best friend broke her promise to keep a secret.)

Say: **In this game, we were afraid of dropping the ball, so we all blew hard to keep it on top of the table. Today we're going to talk about keeping promises. Sometimes it's easy to keep our promises, and sometimes it's hard. But ✦ God wants us to keep our promises. When we break our promises, people can be hurt. So we're going to learn how to keep from dropping the ball when we make promises to others.**

Teacher Tip
Tell children not to mention names of people during this discussion.

**THE POINT**

BIBLE EXPLORATION & APPLICATION

BOAZ MARRIES RUTH 📖

(up to 10 minutes)

Have children act out the story as you tell it. It's OK if girls play boys' parts. Assign the following roles.

- Boaz
- Naomi
- Ruth
- close relative
- city leaders

If you have more than 10 children, have some of the children represent the city gate by standing across from each other and joining hands over their heads as if they are playing London Bridge. Tell Boaz and the close relative to make gestures to each other during their talking parts.

Say: **Today's story comes from Ruth 4:1-15.** Show children the story in the Bible. Keep your Bible open while you tell this story.

Say: **Boaz promised Ruth that he would find out if her closer relative would marry her. If the relative didn't want to marry her, then Boaz had promised that he would marry Ruth. The day after Boaz made the promise, he went and sat by the city gate to wait for the close relative to pass by.** Pause.

As soon as the relative walked by the gate, Boaz called out, "Come here and sit by me, friend." Pause. **So the man came over and sat down by Boaz.** Pause. **Then Boaz gathered some of the city leaders and had them sit down, too.** Pause.

Then Boaz said to the relative, "Naomi wants to sell some land that belonged to her husband. If you want it, buy it now. If you don't want it, tell me because I'd like to buy it and I'm next in line for it after you."

The relative said, "I'd like to buy the land."

Then Boaz said, "If you buy the land, you also have to marry Ruth, Naomi's daughter-in-law. That way the land will stay in their family."

The relative answered, "I can't buy back the land then. If I spend my money on it, but it still belongs to Ruth and Naomi's family, then I won't have enough left for my own family. You'll have to buy it yourself."

Then the relative took off his shoe and gave it to Boaz. Pause. **In Bible times, that meant that he was giving the land to Boaz to buy.**

Then Boaz said to the city leaders, "You are witnesses that I'm buying this land and will marry Ruth so the land stays in her family."

Boaz and Ruth were married (pause to have Boaz and Ruth stand next to each other), **and soon afterward they had a baby boy. Naomi held the**

KEY VERSE Connection

"Sow for yourselves righteousness, reap the fruit of unfailing love, and break up your unplowed ground; for it is time to seek the Lord, until he comes and showers righteousness on you" (Hosea 10:12).

Ruth kept her promise to Naomi. Boaz kept his promise to Ruth. Use this Key Verse to emphasize to your children that God keeps his promises, too, and will pour his goodness on his people like water.

BIBLE INSIGHT

A wedding was a festive event, with the celebration sometimes lasting for a week or more. A parade usually preceded the wedding. The bride and her attendants would walk from her home, and the bridegroom from a place of his choosing. The destination was the groom's father's home. The parade consisted of friends and relatives making music and scattering flowers.

 **THE POINT**

baby in her arms. Pause to have Naomi pretend to hold a baby. **Everyone said, "Praise God. Ruth is a good daughter-in-law because she has given birth to a grandson for Naomi."** Ruth had fulfilled her promise to take care of Naomi, because from then on Boaz and Ruth provided everything Naomi needed. Ask:

● **Sometimes people make promises without meaning to keep them. What would've happened if Boaz had promised to marry Ruth but never intended to do it?** (God would've been unhappy; Ruth would have been mad; Ruth wouldn't have been able to take care of Naomi.)

● **Sometimes people make promises, and then they forget to keep them. What would've happened if Boaz had forgotten his promise to marry Ruth or if Ruth had forgotten her promise to stay with Naomi?** (They would have disappointed God; it would have still been a broken promise; Naomi would have had no one to take care of her.)

Say: **Listen to what the Bible says about promises. Listen for what you should do when you make a promise.** Read **Ecclesiastes 5:4-5.** Ask:

● **What should you do if you make a promise?** (You should keep it; you shouldn't make it if you're not going to keep it.)

Say: **Promises are very important. Boaz and Ruth knew that, and they were very careful to keep the promises they made. That made God happy because ★ God wants us to keep our promises. In fact, the Bible says it's better not to make a promise if we won't be able to keep it. A promise is a promise, and we should always keep our promises just as Boaz and Ruth did.**

TALL TALES 📖

(up to 10 minutes)

Say: **Now we're going to write a tall tale—a story that is so ridiculous it couldn't possibly be true. I'm going to ask you for several words. Then I'll read the story that we've written.**

Ask children to supply the story words for the box on the following page. Then write the words in the appropriate blanks in "The Adventure" (p. 56). When all the blanks are filled in, read "The Adventure" to the children.

Story Words

name for a pet

girl's name

kind of animal

three kinds of food

something really big

game

number

something else really big

another number

After the story, say: **That was a pretty silly story. No one would believe that a boy could meet** (animals) **in the woods that were as big as** (something really big). **Tall tales are funny because we know that what's in them can't possibly be true. Sometimes, though, people make promises that are like tall tales.** Ask:

● **What could someone promise that they couldn't possibly do?** (To turn the sun purple; to drink the whole ocean; to grow another head.)

Say: **Everyone knows not to believe those kinds of promises, and no one would make a promise like that and expect to be able to keep it. But sometimes we make promises that we should keep, but we don't really mean to keep them.** Ask:

● **Has anyone ever made a promise to you that you knew he or she wouldn't keep? How did that make you feel?** (Yes, I felt bad because the person didn't like me enough to keep a promise; yes, I felt that I wasn't very important or she would've kept her promise.)

Say: **When people make promises they don't keep, it's like telling a lie. Listen to what the Bible says about telling lies.** Read **Ephesians 4:25** aloud. **God wants us to tell the truth and ★ God wants us to keep our promises.**

Teacher Tip
It's important to say The Point just as it's written in each activity. Repeating The Point over and over will help children remember it and apply it to their lives.

THE POINT

The Adventure

Once upon a time, Zachary and his dog _____ (name for a pet) went into the

woods near their home to explore and to play. They came across a family of

_____ (kind of animal), who were as big as _____ (something really big). The _____ (same animals)

loved to play _____ (game). When Zachary and _____ (dog's name) saw the

_____ (animals), they stood still, and their mouths dropped open.

The _____ (animals) were outside playing their favorite game, _____ (game).

When the _____ (animals) looked up from their game and saw Zachary and

_____ (dog's name), they jumped up from their game and ran to hide behind the

trees even though they were as big as _____ (something else really big). Zachary could clearly

see them shaking in fear. So Zachary said, "Don't be scared. We want to be friends."

Finally the _____ (animals) crept out from behind the trees. One of them

came close to Zachary and _____ (dog's name). The _____ (animal) shyly

said, "How do you do? I'm _____ (girl's name). Would you like to come inside

our home? It's almost time for tea."

Zachary agreed because he was very hungry after his hike into the woods. So

Zachary, _____ (dog's name), and the _____ (animals) all went inside for tea.

Teatime was very joyous for the _____ (animals). They loved to eat, and they'd

worked up quite an appetite playing _____ (game) along with the tea. They were all so hungry that

served _____ (three kinds of food) along with the tea. They were all so hungry that

they ate _____ (number) tons of food and drank _____ (another number) gallons of tea.

Then Zachary said, "Thank you so much. It's time for us to go home now." And

he and _____ (dog's name) shook hands with everyone and walked home. As

they walked home, they decided to keep their adventure a secret.

PROMISE BOUQUETS 📖

(up to 15 minutes)

Before class place a sheet of the *flower foam* on a photocopier, and make a photocopy for each child. Each child should get a sheet with nine flowers on it.

Say: **When we keep our promises to others, it makes them feel special and cared for. Let's make bouquets of promises to make others feel good.**

Hand out the photocopies, and have the children cut out the flowers and think of promises they can make. They can think of several promises for one person, or they can think of promises they can make to different people. Have children write words or draw pictures of those promises on the flowers. Then have each child glue or tape the flowers to a sheet of construction paper and use markers to add stems and leaves.

While the children are working, ask:

● **How do you feel when someone keeps a promise to you?** (Good; important; loved.)

● **What can you do to make sure you keep your promises?** (Write them down; only make promises I know I can keep; ask someone to help me remember.)

● **Sometimes, no matter how hard we try, we break a promise. What can we do when we break a promise?** (Say we're sorry; explain what happened; do something nice to make it up to the person.)

When children complete their promise bouquets, have them share their promises with the rest of the class.

Say: **Special people keep their promises. Each one of you can keep the promises you make. But everyone makes mistakes. Sometimes we break our promises. If that happens to us, we can say, "I'm sorry," because we know that breaking promises hurts others. Take your pictures home, and put them where you'll see them often. This bouquet is for you.**

When you see this bouquet, remember that ★ God wants you to keep your promises. The Bible says in Proverbs 12:22b, "The Lord...is pleased with those who keep their promises" (New Century Version). **You can pretend that you're giving someone a beautiful bouquet of flowers each time you keep a promise.**

THE POINT ★

We believe that Christian education extends beyond the classroom into the home. **GROWING TOGETHER** Photocopy the "Growing Together" handout (p. 59) for this week, and send it home with your children. Encourage children and parents to use the handout to plan meaningful activities on this week's topic. Follow up the "Growing Together" activities next week by asking children what their families did together.

CLOSING

TRUST ME

(up to 10 minutes)

Ask:

● **What did you learn today?** (I learned that promises are special; I learned to keep my promises; I learned that God wants me to keep promises.)

Give each child a Tootsie Pop lollipop. Say: **When you unwrap your lollipop, you can't see into the middle to know that there's Tootsie Roll candy in the middle, but the company that makes them promises that candy is in the middle of every lollipop. People are the same. You can't look inside them to know for sure if they're promise keepers. You have to trust that people will keep their promises. Let's agree to be the kind of people who can be trusted to keep their promises, because ⭐ God wants us to keep our promises.**

Say: **In our story, Boaz took off his shoe to show that he promised to buy Ruth's land and marry her. Today we might cross our hearts to show that we've made a promise. Let's cross our hearts to everyone else in the room to show that we want to keep our promises.**

Give children time to do this. Then pray and ask for God's help in being promise keepers.

RUTH 4:

God wants us to keep our promises.

KEY VERSE

"Sow for yourselves right-eousness, reap the fruit of unfailing love, and break up your unplowed ground; for it is time to seek the Lord, until he comes and showers righteousness on you" (Hosea 10:12).

GROWING TOGETHER

I·N T·O·U·C·H

Today your child learned that God is pleased when we keep our promises. The children learned to be careful not to make rash promises because we show others how much we care for them when we keep our promises. The children also learned that a broken promise is like a lie. Use these activities at home to teach your child the importance of keeping his or her promises.

A JOINT PROMISE

Make a promise with your child this week, and keep it faithfully. For example, you might promise each other to pray together before you leave the house in the morning. Or you might promise to spend a half-hour together each evening reading, talking, or exercising. At the end of the week, celebrate your faithfulness by watching a movie together or going out for frozen yogurt. Give your child another promise—tell your child that your love for him or her will last forever.

A PERFECT EXAMPLE

Take turns thinking of promises that God has made. For example, God promised to give Abraham and Sarah a child, and God promised Noah to never again destroy the earth in a flood. Also think of promises that God has made that haven't come true yet. For example, Jesus promised to come again. See if you can come up with three promises each night this week. Every night, thank God for being a perfect example of a promise keeper. Tell God that you trust that all of his promises will come true. Promise God to be faithful in keeping your promises.

FORGOTTEN COOKIES

Set out 3 egg whites until they reach room temperature. To the egg whites, add ¼ teaspoon mint extract, ¼ teaspoon cream of tartar, and a dash of salt. Beat to soft peaks. Gradually add 1 cup sugar, beating until stiff, glossy peaks form. Gently fold in 1 cup mini–chocolate chips and green food coloring (optional). Cover a baking sheet with plain, ungreased brown paper. Drop the meringue by teaspoonfuls onto the paper. Bake at 275° for 1 hour. Then turn off the heat, and let dry in oven (with the door closed) for at least 2 hours. Take the cookies out of the oven, and store them in an airtight container. While you enjoy the treats, talk about how God wants us to keep our promises even when no one's looking—just as the cookies kept baking even though you turned off the oven and "forgot" about them.

BROKEN PROMISES

Place two toothpicks side by side in a bowl of water. Dip the tip of a third tooth-pick in liquid dishwashing detergent. Then touch the water between the sticks with the third toothpick. The two floating tooth-picks will quickly move away from each other. Talk about the trouble that broken promises can cause between friends and family members.

D·A·V·I·D

When God revealed his plan for David to lead Israel, David was still a boy. Neither Samuel nor Jesse nor any of David's older brothers could have known the incredible future that God had in store for the youngster. David became a man of strength and intelligence. He was loved by the people, and he was a man after God's own heart. He was an accomplished musician. He is the best-known poet of all time. He was Israel's shining king, yet David began his career as a humble servant and an obedient child.

The lessons in this module will teach children about David's life before his amazing kingship began. The story of David offers an exceptional example of how to trust and follow God. These lessons about the life of young David will help first- and second-graders recognize that God will provide a way for them to meet the challenges they will face every day. They don't have to wait until they're grown up—they can live faithfully right now. In this module, children will learn that God looks at inner character rather than outer appearance, that God gives us strength to do impossible tasks, that God wants us to be kind to others no matter how they treat us, and that God wants us to act wisely.

FOUR LESSONS ON DAVID			
LESSON	**PAGE**	**THE POINT**	**THE BIBLE BASIS**
5—GOD SEES MY HEART	65	God doesn't judge us by the way we look.	1 Samuel 16:1-13
6—GOD GIVES STRENGTH	75	God can help us do things that seem impossible.	1 Samuel 17:1-51
7—ALWAYS KIND	83	God helps us be kind, even when people are mean to us.	1 Samuel 24:1-22
8—BE WISE	93	God wants us to act wisely.	1 Samuel 25:1-35

THE SIGNAL

During the lessons on David, your attention-getting signal will be clapping your hands three times. Have children respond by clapping their hands three times as they stop talking and focus their attention on you. Tell children about this signal before the lesson begins. Explain that it's important to respond to this signal quickly so the class can do as many fun activities as possible.

THE FIDGET BUSTER

When your students are too antsy to pay attention to the lesson, play this game to get the wiggles out.

Say: **When David was a boy, his job was to take care of sheep. Let's pretend we're sheep in this game. Sheep like to follow the crowd, so in this game we're all going to imitate each other. Each person will get a chance to choose an action, and we'll all follow you.**

Have children stand in a circle and begin walking to the right. Call out a child's name, and have him or her choose an action for the class to imitate, such as hopping on one leg around the circle or walking backward. After a few seconds, call out another child's name, and have the class follow his or her action. Continue until each child has had a chance to be the leader.

Then say: **Now it's my turn to be the leader. Sheep, follow me back to our lesson.**

THE TIME STUFFER

The Time Stuffer for the four lessons on David is a poster titled "Growing Up Godly." It will help children learn that they can do great things to please God now, just as young David did. Hang the poster at eye level, and put paper and markers nearby. Any time children come to class early or finish an activity before others, have them read the poster and draw pictures of themselves doing great things for God.

 REMEMBERING GOD'S WORD

Each four- or five-week module focuses on a Key Bible Verse. The Key Verse for this module is "Don't let anyone look down on you because you are young, but set an example for the believers in speech, in life, in love, in faith and in purity" **(1 Timothy 4:12).**

This module's Key Verse will teach children that their actions and words are as important as adults'. God calls all people to faithful obedience no matter what their ages are. Have fun using these ideas any time during the lessons on David.

And look for the Key Verse Connection in the margin of each lesson. It will help you tie the module's Key Verse to The Point of the lesson.

KIDS CAN!

LEARNING LAB

Hang two sheets of newsprint on a wall in your classroom. At the top of one sheet write "Grown-Ups." At the top of the other write "Kids." Ask:

● **What can grown-ups do that kids don't do?** (Go to work; stay up late; eat ice cream whenever they want.)

Write children's answers on the "Grown-Ups" newsprint. Then ask:

● **What do kids do that grown-ups don't do?** (Play on the playground; go to elementary school; go on kiddie rides at the fair.)

Write children's answers on the "Kids" newsprint. If children have trouble thinking of answers to this question, suggest rolling down hills, hanging upside down on monkey bars, and giggling. Ask:

● **Would you rather be a kid or a grown-up? Explain.** (A grown-up, because they get to make the rules; a kid, because we have more fun.)

Say: **It's great to be a grown-up, and it's great to be a kid. Young people can do important things for God. Listen to what the Bible says about young people.** Read **1 Timothy 4:12.** Ask:

● **What can kids do for God?** (Tell other kids about God; read the Bible; go to church; do good things for each other.)

Read **1 Timothy 4:12** again, and have children repeat the verse with you. Say: **Let's give a cheer for young people who want to be examples for God.**

Teach the children this cheer. The cheer is on the *cassette tape* to help you learn the clapping rhythm. The tape segment is titled **"1 Timothy 4:12."**

Teacher Tip

If boys are reluctant to act like cheerleaders, tell them that some of the best college cheerleaders are boys because they're strong enough to do super jumps and they can shout loudly.

I am not a nobody because I am so young.
(clap   clap)

I will be a role model to those who love the Lord.
(clap   clap)

They will see my words,
(stomp   stomp   clap   clap)

(continued)

my actions,
(stomp   stomp   clap   clap)

my love,
(stomp   stomp   clap   clap)

my faith,
(stomp   stomp   clap   clap)

pure life.
(stomp   stomp   clap   clap)

EXAMPLES OF FAITH

LEARNING LAB

Trace the *foam person* on a sheet of paper. It will fit if you tilt it slightly. Use legal-sized paper if it's available. Photocopy the tracing for each child.

Say: **Let's talk about being examples. Listen to what the Bible says about being an example. Listen for who can be an example.** Read **1 Timothy 4:12.** Have children repeat the verse with you. Ask:

● **Who can be an example?** (I can; young people; kids.)

● **What can you be an example of?** (Being a good Christian; doing good; obeying.)

Distribute the photocopies of the tracing. Provide markers or crayons. Say: **Decorate this person to look like yourself.**

Give children five minutes to decorate the outlines. While the children are working, ask:

● **Who can you be an example to?** (My neighbors; my cousins; my friends; my family.)

● **What can you do to be an example?** (Obey; follow the Bible; go to church; tell others about Jesus.)

When the children are finished decorating, have them write **"1 Timothy 4:12"** on the top of their papers and repeat the verse with you. Then have them write words or draw pictures that describe people who are good examples.

Read the verse again, and have children say it with you. Say: **Each of you can be an example of godliness. You're already an example because you came to class today. Keep up the good work!**

G·O·D S·E·E·S M·Y H·E·A·R·T

THE POINT
God doesn't judge us by the way we look.

THE BIBLE BASIS:
1 Samuel 16:1-13. Samuel anoints David.

Samuel took the time to listen to God. Even so, when God told him to anoint the next king of Israel, Samuel assumed that God would choose a man who would be strong and impressive like Saul. Samuel was wowed by the strength and appearance of Jesse's older sons. But God quickly reminded Samuel that an individual's inner character is more important than physical appearance.

First- and second-graders are learning to make good decisions. It's easy for children to make choices based on what *looks* good to them. But often, looks are deceiving. The adage "Don't judge a book by its cover" is good advice for children. It's good news, too, because God doesn't judge us by our looks. He delves deep into our hearts. God knows our motives, our intentions, and our desires. God created us in his image so that no matter what we look like, we can be assured that God created us deliberately to be the way we are. Teach your children that God cares about what's inside of them more than he cares about how they look.

Other Scriptures used in this lesson are **Psalm 139:13-16** and **Hebrews 4:13.**

KEY VERSE
for Lessons 5–8

"Don't let anyone look down on you because you are young, but set an example for the believers in speech, in life, in love, in faith and in purity" (1 Timothy 4:12).

GETTING THE POINT

Children will

- realize that God knows more about them than they know about themselves,
- discover that judging by appearances can lead to disappointment, and
- learn that God can make something special out of something ordinary.

Before the lesson, collect the items from the Learning Lab for the activities you plan to use. Refer to the pictures in the margin to see what each item looks like.

THIS LESSON AT A GLANCE

SECTION	MINUTES	WHAT CHILDREN WILL DO	LEARNING LAB SUPPLIES	CLASSROOM SUPPLIES
WELCOME TIME	up to 5	**Welcome!**—Receive a warm welcome from the teacher and make name tags.		"Outside-Inside Name Tags" (p. 73), scissors, markers, tape or safety pins
ATTENTION GRABBER	up to 10	**What Does It Do?**—Think of games to play with a wheel and learn that the wheel can do more than they think it can.	Super bouncing wheel	Paper, pencil
BIBLE EXPLORATION & APPLICATION	up to 12	**Who Are We?**—Design costumes and a personality for the foam person and talk about the qualities inside that make each individual special.	Felt strips, plastic rings, glitter pins, flower foam, foam person	Bible, colored paper, markers, scissors
	up to 15	**David Is Anointed**—Act out 1 Samuel 16:1-13 in which God chooses David as the next king of Israel.	Foam person	Bible, scissors, paper, marker
	up to 10	**Only God Knows**—Search for answers, hear Hebrews 4:13, and learn that only God knows everything about us.		Bible, index cards, pencils, tape
CLOSING	up to 8	**Outside-Inside Hearts**—Share about the special things each one has inside, hear Psalm 139:14, and thank God for looking beyond the way they look to see what's in their hearts.		Bible

Remember to make photocopies of the "Growing Together" handout (p. 74) to send home with your children. "Growing Together" is a valuable tool for helping first- and second-graders talk with their parents about what they're learning in class.

T·H·E L·E·S·S·O·N

WELCOME TIME

WELCOME!
(up to 5 minutes)

- Greet each child individually with an enthusiastic smile.
- Thank each child for coming to class today.
- As children arrive, ask them about last week's "Growing Together" discussion. Use questions such as "What promise did you and your family make? How did you celebrate keeping your promise?" and "What are some promises that God makes to you?"
- Say: **Today we're going to learn that**  **God doesn't judge us by the way we look.**
- Help children make name tags. Photocopy the "Outside-Inside Name Tags" (p. 73), and follow the instructions.
- Tell children that the attention-getting signal you'll use during this lesson is clapping your hands three times. Ask children to respond by clapping their hands three times as they stop talking and focus their attention on you. Rehearse the signal with the children, telling them to respond quickly so you have plenty of time for all the fun activities planned for this lesson.

THE POINT ★

ATTENTION GRABBER

WHAT DOES IT DO?
(up to 10 minutes)

Have children sit in a circle. Pass around the *super bouncing wheel,* and let each child look at it and feel it.

Say: **It would be fun to play a game with this wheel. Let's see how many ideas we can think of to do with it. I'll write down all your ideas. What can we do with this wheel?**

Have children think of ideas such as finding out who can roll it the farthest or who can bounce it the highest. Write down each idea, and be sure you use a pencil instead of a pen. When the children have thought of several ideas, misspell a word, and say: **Oh, no! I made a mistake. Now I need an eraser.** Suggest

LEARNING LAB

Teacher Tip

If you have time, play one of the games the children thought of.

THE POINT

using the wheel as an eraser. Erase the misspelled word with the wheel.

Say: **This *super bouncing wheel* has a hidden talent. Most people wouldn't expect a toy wheel to be an eraser, too. You know, I have a hidden talent, and I bet each of you has a hidden talent too.** Ask:

● **Can you guess my hidden talent?** (Share with the children a special talent you have, such as decorating cakes or playing softball.)

Say: **In just a moment, we'll talk about your hidden talents. Today's lesson is good news because** ★ **God doesn't judge us by the way we look. God cares about what's inside each of us. God cares about our thoughts and our feelings. Today we're going to learn about the special traits and talents that we have hidden inside us. Let's find out more.**

Return the *super bouncing wheel* to the Learning Lab.

BIBLE EXPLORATION & APPLICATION

WHO ARE WE? 📖

(up to 12 minutes)

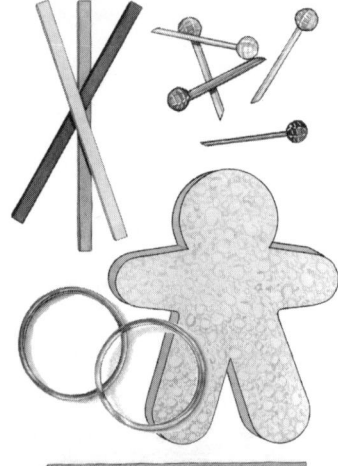

LEARNING LAB

Form groups of three. Give each group some of the *felt strips, glitter pins, flower foam,* a *plastic ring,* colored paper, markers, and scissors. Put the *foam person* on a table where everyone can see it.

Say: **This *foam person* doesn't have much of a personality right now—it doesn't even have a face. Let's create costumes for the person that show who it is and what it's interested in. You'll decide if the person is a boy or a girl, what it looks like, and what its interests and hobbies are. You'll have five minutes to work. Then each group will attach its costume to the *foam person* with the *glitter pins* and tell us about its interests and hobbies.**

Give the children five minutes to work. While they're working, ask questions such as "What name have you given the person?" "How old is the person?" "What does the person like to do?" "What job does the person have?"

After five minutes, call time by clapping your hands three times to get children's attention. Wait for the children to respond by clapping three times and focusing their attention on you.

Have each group put its costume on the *foam person* and tell the class about its personality. Encourage the rest of the class to ask questions about the person.

Say: **It was fun to decide what this person looks like, and it was even more fun to decide what it likes to do. God decided what we would look like. And what's even more important, God decided what we'd be like on the inside, too. Listen to what the Bible says about God making us.** Read **Psalm 139:13, 15-16** aloud. **God made us just the way he wants us to be. God has given each of us lots of interesting qualities and special talents.**

Ask:

● **What's an interesting quality or special talent you have?** (I can wiggle my ears; I can play the piano; I'm a good soccer player.)

● **What's your favorite thing to do?** (Watch TV; play video games; play football; play with my Barbie dolls.)

● **What's your favorite thing to eat?** (Pizza; tacos; spaghetti; brownies.)

● **What do you want to be when you grow up?** (A lawyer; an astronaut; a basketball player; the president.)

Say: **God made each of us. Look around the room. Each person looks different from everybody else. Even twins look a little bit different, because we can tell them apart. But ★ God doesn't judge us by the way we look. God looks at what's inside of us. We're all different on the inside, too. It's what's inside us that makes us special. We're going to learn about the time God showed Samuel how he looks inside people's hearts.**

THE POINT ★

DAVID IS ANOINTED 📖

(up to 15 minutes)

Cut a sheet of paper into seven strips. Write "Son #1" on one strip, "Son #2" on another, "Son #3" on another, and so on until all seven strips are labeled with "Son #1" through "Son #7."

Have children sit in a circle. Pass out the seven strips of paper to the first seven children, and have them put the strips on the floor in front of them. Have the next child in the circle be Samuel, and have the next person be David.

Say: **If you have a slip of paper, you'll need to know these actions. When it's your turn, the class will say, "He's tall," and you'll lift your hand up in the air. Let's practice that. Class, say, "He's tall."** Pause to practice the action. **Then the class will say, "He's handsome," and you'll wave your hand in a circle around your face. Let's practice that. Class, say, "He's handsome."** Pause. **Then the class will say, "He must be the one," and you'll pound your fist in your hand. Let's practice that. Class, say, "He must be the one."** Pause.

To Samuel say: **Every time you hear the word "Samuel," cup one hand to your ear to show that Samuel listened to God.**

To David say: **Every time you hear the word "David," make trickling motions over your head and face with your fingers to show that David's head was anointed with oil.**

Give the *foam person* to the child with the slip labeled "Son #1." Open your Bible to **1 Samuel 16:1-13,** and show the passage to the children.

Say: **One day, God said to the prophet Samuel (pause), "I am sending you to Jesse's house in Bethlehem. He has many sons, and I have chosen one of them to become the next king of Israel."**

Samuel (pause) listened and obeyed God. He took a young calf for a sacrifice and a container of olive oil and started out for Bethlehem.

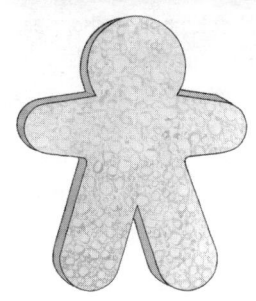

Teacher Tip
If you have fewer than nine children in class, allow students to play more than one role during this activity.

When Samuel (pause) **arrived, he found Jesse and said, "I'm going to offer a sacrifice. Come and bring your sons to the feast."**

When Jesse and his sons came to the sacrifice, Jesse presented the first son to Samuel (pause). Samuel (pause) **thought, "Surely God has chosen this young man."** Have the first child do the actions while the class says, "He's tall (pause). He's handsome (pause). He must be the one (pause)."

But God said, "Don't look at how handsome or tall Eliab is. I haven't chosen him to be the new king."

Jesse presented another son. Give the *foam person* to Son #2. Have the second child do the actions while the class says, "He's tall (pause). He's handsome (pause). He must be the one (pause)."

But Samuel (pause) **said again, "God hasn't chosen this man."**

Jesse presented another son. Give the *foam person* to Son #3. Have the third child do the actions while the class says, "He's tall (pause). He's handsome (pause). He must be the one (pause)."

But Samuel (pause) **said again, "God hasn't chosen this man."**

Jesse presented another son. Give the *foam person* to Son #4. Have the fourth child do the actions while the class says, "He's tall (pause). He's handsome (pause). He must be the one (pause)."

But Samuel (pause) **said again, "God hasn't chosen this man."**

Jesse presented another son. Give the *foam person* to Son #5. Have the fifth child do the actions while the class says, "He's tall (pause). He's handsome (pause). He must be the one (pause)."

But Samuel (pause) **said again, "God hasn't chosen this man."**

Jesse presented another son. Give the *foam person* to Son #6. Have the sixth child do the actions while the class says, "He's tall (pause). He's handsome (pause). He must be the one (pause)."

But Samuel (pause) **said again, "God hasn't chosen this man."**

Jesse presented another son. Give the *foam person* to Son #7. Have the seventh child do the actions while the class says, "He's tall (pause). He's handsome (pause). He must be the one (pause)."

But Samuel (pause) **said again, "God hasn't chosen this man."**

Seven sons were presented to Samuel (pause), **and seven times Samuel** (pause) **said, "No, this isn't the right one."**

Samuel (pause) **asked, "Are these all the sons you have?"**

Jesse said, "I still have the youngest son. He is out taking care of the sheep."

Samuel (pause) **said, "Send for the boy. We won't sit down to eat until he comes."**

Jesse sent for his youngest son. When David (pause) **came into the room, God said to Samuel** (pause), **"Go and anoint him, because he is the one I want to be king of Israel."**

Samuel (pause) **took the container of olive oil and poured it on David** (pause) **to anoint him. From that day on God's Spirit worked in David** (pause). Ask:

● **Why do you think God chose David to be the next king of Israel?**

BIBLE INSIGHT

When he arrived at Jesse's home to anoint the next king, Samuel favored Jesse's eldest son, Eliab. But God taught Samuel to look for inner, rather than outer, qualities. It is thought that Jesse and his family may not have understood the future implications of David's anointing.

(Because God knew that David was the best person; because God knew all about David.)

Say:  **God doesn't judge us by the way we look. God picked David to be the next king even though David was the youngest and the littlest of Jesse's sons. God picked David because David was the best one for the job. Now let's talk about what God knows about you.**

ONLY GOD KNOWS 📖

(up to 10 minutes)

Give each person an index card and a pencil. Have each child secretly write a word or draw a picture on the card. Then form pairs, and have children tape their cards face down on their partners' backs without telling what's written on the cards.

Say: **Your job is to find out what is written on the card that's taped to your back. Search for clues by asking anyone in the room to help you figure it out. You may not lift your card or anyone else's card. You'll have a minute to figure out what's on your card.**

Let the children ask each other for clues for one minute. If someone figures out that his or her partner is the only person he or she can get an answer from, stop the game. Gather the children on the floor, and ask:

● **What clues did your classmates give you?** (They couldn't tell me anything; all they said was the card was blank.)

● **Who was the only person in the room who knew what was written on the card that was taped to your back?** (My partner; the person who wrote on the card; I don't know.)

Say: **Only the person who gave you the card knew what was written on it. In the same way, only God, the one who made you, knows everything about you. God knows us even better than we know ourselves. Listen to what the Bible says about how well God knows us.** Read **Hebrews 4:13.**

Say: **God knows what we're like on the inside. He can look inside our hearts and minds where no one else can see.**  **God doesn't judge us by the way we look. God looks at what's inside us. He knows the good thoughts we have and the bad thoughts we have.**

Have children take off their cards and throw them away.

> ### Teacher Tip
> It's important to say The Point just as it's written in each activity. Repeating The Point over and over will help children remember it and apply it to their lives.

We believe that Christian education extends beyond the classroom into the home. **GROWING TOGETHER** Photocopy the "Growing Together" handout (p. 74) for this week, and send it home with your children. Encourage children and parents to use the handout to plan meaningful activities on this week's topic. Follow up the "Growing Together" activities next week by asking children what their families did together.

CLOSING

OUTSIDE-INSIDE HEARTS 📖
(up to 8 minutes)

Ask:

● **What did you learn today?** (I learned that God knows what I'm thinking; I learned that God made me; I learned that God doesn't judge me by the way I look.)

Have the children sit in a circle. Say: **Today we talked about how God looks at what's inside of us. The Bible calls that place the heart. It's the place inside us where we think and feel. To remind you of the place inside of you, I'm going to show you a heart that you can see.** Use the margin diagram to guide you in making a heart with your hands. **Place the fingernails of one hand against the fingernails of your other hand. Now cup your hands so that the heels of your hands touch. See the heart shape?**

Say: **There's a space inside of the heart that you make with your hands. Let's pretend that space is where God looks. Let's talk about the things we have inside our hearts that please God.**

Start with the child on your left. Have the child hold out his or her heart shape. Have the other children mention inner qualities the child has that please God, such as being helpful or cheerful. As the children mention those inner qualities, have them pretend to tuck the qualities inside the child's heart shape. Repeat this process for every child in the circle. Think of at least one quality for each child in case the rest of the class can't think of anything. It's OK if the same quality is mentioned more than once.

Say: **Any time you need to remember how special you are, make the heart shape with your hands and remember what your classmates told you about what's inside you. Listen to what the Bible says about how special you are.**

Read **Psalm 139:14.** Then pray: **God, we're thankful that ✦ you don't judge us by the way we look. We know that you've made us exactly the way you want us. Help us to please you with what we do and with what we think. In Jesus' name, amen.**

✦ **THE POINT**

OUTSIDE-INSIDE NAME TAGS

Photocopy this handout so there is one pattern for each child. Each handout contains two patterns. Cut the handouts in half vertically to separate the patterns. Have children cut out the patterns on the bold lines. On the inside of the hearts, have children write something that's special about them-selves. Then have them fold the flaps so that special thing is hidden—this becomes the back of the name tag. Have children turn the heart over and write their names on the outside of the heart.

DAVID 5:

God doesn't judge us by the way we look.

KEY VERSE

"Don't let anyone look down on you because you are young, but set an example for the believers in speech, in life, in love, in faith and in purity" (1 Timothy 4:12).

GROWING TOGETHER

Today your child learned that God looks past our appearance to what's in our hearts. The children learned that God made them with special talents and abilities and that God knows everything about them. Use these activities to teach your child that what we are inside is what matters to God.

SHARED SECRETS

· · · · · · ·

Read 1 Samuel 16:7b with your child. Then spend time together so your child knows what's hidden in your heart. Take time to share secrets with your child. Talk about your favorite foods and your favorite colors. Talk about your favorite pastimes and your wildest dreams. Read your favorite childhood books to your child. Ask your child what's been on his or her heart. Enjoy getting to know your child as an individual.

PLAIN OLD ROCKS?

· · · · · · · · · · ·

Take your child to a store that sells polished rocks, visit the rocks and minerals section of a museum, or check out a book about rocks from your local library. Compare how rocks and gems look before and after they're polished. Talk to your child about potential—a rockhound knows how pretty a plain rock will be once it's polished. God knows how beautiful we can be, so he works in us. Compare the inside of a geode to the outside. A geode looks like a plain, round rock on the outside, but there are beautiful crystals on the inside. Talk to your child about hidden abilities and talents. Collect an assortment of rocks with your child as a reminder that God knows our potential and he knows how beautiful we are on the inside.

GIFTS GALORE

· · · · · · · · · · ·

Buy identical gifts, such as a candy bar that everyone likes, for each member of the family. Have your child decorate lunch bags to be used as gift bags for the gifts. At least one bag should be decorated beautifully. At least one of the bags should look as ugly as possible—your child could crumple it into a wad. Put a gift into each bag, and staple each bag shut. Gather your family, and have one family member choose a bag without opening it or shaking it. The next family member can take that bag or choose any of the other bags. Continue until everyone has a bag. Then open the bags. Talk about looking beyond appearances to what people have inside.

HIDDEN TREASURE

· · · · · · · · · · ·

Line the bottom and sides of small, clear glasses or bowls with whipped dessert topping. Mix your family's favorite pudding with small candies. Nestle spoonfuls of the pudding mixture in the topping-lined bowls, and cover with another layer of the whipped topping. Serve the dessert to your family, and talk about the treasures that each member of your family has inside.

G·O·D G·I·V·E·S S·T·R·E·N·G·T·H

THE POINT
God can help us do things that seem impossible.

THE BIBLE BASIS:
1 Samuel 17:1-51. David fights Goliath.

David was able to conquer Goliath because David depended on God's strength. Although David was young, God had proven himself to David over and over. Ferocious lions and bears threatened the sheep that David was in charge of, yet God always gave him the strength to defeat the predators. David had no doubt that God would be with him when he faced the giant, even though the trained soldiers in Saul's army were quaking with fear.

The giants that first- and second-graders face aren't 9-foot monsters. They're bullies on the playground, frustrating home situations, challenging schoolwork, and ungodly values. To conquer these challenges, children need strength and faith. Strengthen your students' faith by teaching them about the small shepherd boy who accomplished the impossible with God's help.

Isaiah 41:10 is also used in this lesson.

KEY VERSE
for Lessons 5–8

"Don't let anyone look down on you because you are young, but set an example for the believers in speech, in life, in love, in faith and in purity" (1 Timothy 4:12).

GETTING THE POINT

Children will

- learn that God is strong and powerful and will help them slay giants in their own lives,
- discover that God promises to be with them all the time, and
- write poems about situations in which God will help them.

Before the lesson, collect the items from the Learning Lab for the activities you plan to use. Refer to the pictures in the margin to see what each item looks like.

THIS LESSON AT A GLANCE

SECTION	MINUTES	WHAT CHILDREN WILL DO	LEARNING LAB SUPPLIES	CLASSROOM SUPPLIES
WELCOME TIME	up to 5	**Welcome!**—Receive a warm welcome from the teacher and make name tags.		"Outside-Inside Name Tags" (p. 73), scissors, markers, tape or safety pins
ATTENTION GRABBER	up to 10	**Hoop Shoot**—Throw plastic rings toward a small target and talk about the hard tasks they face in life.	Darts, plastic rings	
BIBLE EXPLORATION & APPLICATION	up to 15	**The Boy and the Giant**—Listen to the story of David and Goliath from 1 Samuel 17:1-51 and learn that God will give them strength to do the impossible.	Cassette: "The Boy and the Giant"	Bible, cassette player
	up to 10	**Always There**—Draw a picture with taped-together crayons, hear Isaiah 41:10, and learn that God is always with them to give them strength to do difficult things.		Bible, crayons, tape, paper
	up to 10	**The Lion and the Bear**—Write poems based on 1 Samuel 17:37 that recognize God's help in the past and acknowledge God's help for the future.		Bible, newsprint, marker
CLOSING	up to 10	**Giant Slayers**—Knock over a giant that represents something that's toughest for them to do and learn that God can do anything.	Glitter pins, foam person, squirty fish, Wikki Stix	

Remember to make photocopies of the "Growing Together" handout (p. 82) to send home with your children. "Growing Together" is a valuable tool for helping first- and second-graders talk with their parents about what they're learning in class.

 **ELCOME TIME**

WELCOME!
(up to 5 minutes)

● Greet each child individually with an enthusiastic smile.
● Thank each child for coming to class today.
● As children arrive, ask them about last week's "Growing Together" discussion. Use questions such as "Which gift bag did your family choose first? What did your family learn from the gift-bag activity?" and "How did your hidden-treasure dessert remind you to look for treasures inside of others?"
● Say: **Today we're going to learn that**  **God can help us do things that seem impossible.**

THE POINT ★

● Hand out the name tags children made during Lesson 5, and help children attach the name tags to their clothing. If some of the name tags were damaged, or if children weren't in class that week, have them make new name tags using the photocopiable handout on page 73.
● Tell children that the attention-getting signal you'll use during this lesson is clapping your hands three times. Ask children to respond by clapping their hands three times as they stop talking and focus their attention on you. Rehearse the signal with the children, telling them to respond quickly so you have plenty of time for all the fun activities planned for this lesson.

 **TTENTION GRABBER**

HOOP SHOOT
(up to 10 minutes)

Dampen the suction cups of the *darts,* and press the *darts* to a table top so they stick.

Have the children line up five to 10 feet away from the table. Hand the first child five *plastic rings.* Say: **You'll have 10 seconds to toss the *plastic rings* onto the *darts.***

After the first child has thrown all five rings, have him or her retrieve them

 **LEARNING LAB**

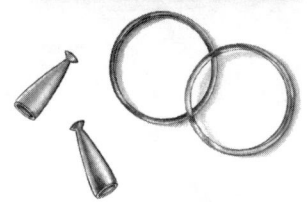

GOD GIVES STRENGTH **77**

and give them to the next child in line. Continue until every child has had a chance to toss the rings. Then gather the rings and the *darts,* and return them to the Learning Lab. Have the children sit down on the floor. Ask:

● **Did you think this game was easy or hard? Explain.** (It was hard because I couldn't get any of the rings to land on the *darts;* it was hard because my aim isn't that good and we didn't have much time.)

● **What did you think about as you waited for your turn?** (I got nervous because it looked so hard; I was excited because I was sure I could do better than some of the others.)

● **Was anyone surprised when you couldn't ring the *darts* with all five of the *plastic rings?*** (No, because it is impossible to do; no, because no one's that good.)

● **What's hard or impossible for you to do in real life?** (Catch a baseball; throw a spiral in football; spelling; subtraction; reading.)

● **What do you do when you come up against a tough challenge?** (I worry; I get scared; I try hard; I ask for help.)

Say: **Everyone faces tough situations every day. Some of those tough situations seem impossible, just as it was impossible to ring the *darts* with all five of the *plastic rings.* The hero of today's Bible story faced a tough challenge that no one else was willing to face. But our hero was sure that he could do it because he knew that God was with him and ✦ God can help us do things that seem impossible. Let's listen and find out what happened.**

THE POINT

BIBLE EXPLORATION & APPLICATION

THE BOY AND THE GIANT 📖

(up to 15 minutes)

LEARNING LAB

Cue the *cassette tape* to the segment titled "The Boy and the Giant." Gather the children and say: **Get in your favorite position for listening.** Open your Bible to **1 Samuel 17:1-51,** and show children the passage. Say: **Even though this story is on the *cassette tape,* it comes from the Bible.** Begin the tape. When the story is over, turn off the cassette player and ask:

● **Do you think David was scared when he went out to fight Goliath? Why or why not?** (No, because he knew God would help him; yes, because Goliath was so big.)

● **Why was David so sure that God would help him?** (Because God had helped him fight a bear and a lion; because David knew that God is strong.)

● **How can you know that God will help you?** (Because my parents tell me God will help; because God helped David; because the Bible promises that God will help me.)

Say: **Even though David was a lot smaller than Goliath, it was easy for David to defeat him. All he did was throw a rock at him.** ✦ **God can help us do things that seem impossible, too. God helped David, and we can know that God will help us because the Bible promises that God will always be there for us. Let's find out about how God stays with us.**

ALWAYS THERE 📖

(up to 10 minutes)

Have each child choose two different-colored crayons and tape the crayons together so the tips are at the same level. Wrap tape around the two crayons along the entire length of the crayons. Hand out paper, and tell the children to draw pictures of themselves facing tough situations. Tell them to try to draw the pictures with both crayon tips touching the paper.

While the children are working, ask:

● **How do you feel when you know you have to do something that seems impossible?** (Scared; worried; excited; like I can't do it.)

● **Who helps you when you have to do something hard? What do they do for you?** (God gives me strength; my mom prays with me; my brother helps me.)

Give the children five to seven minutes to work on their pictures. When they're finished, let them each explain their drawings to the rest of the class.

Say: **Listen to what the Bible says about someone who will help us when times are tough. Listen to what that person will do for you.** Read **Isaiah 41:10.** Ask:

● **Who will help you when times are tough?** (God; the Lord; Jesus.)

● **What will God do for you?** (Help me not to worry; make me strong; stay with me; help me not be afraid; hold me up with his hand.)

Say: **Look at your picture. See the double line that was made by drawing with taped-together crayons? That extra line is to remind you that no matter where you go, God will go with you to give you strength and help you do things that are hard. Take your double crayon, and try to break it in half.** Give children a moment to try it. Some may be able to do it, but it will take some effort.

Say: **It's much tougher to break the double crayon than it is to break a single crayon. That's what happens when God is with us. God makes us stronger.** ✦ **God can help us do things that seem impossible, and God promises to be with us all the time.**

KEY **VERSE** Connection

"Don't let anyone look down on you because you are young, but set an example for the believers in speech, in life, in love, in faith and in purity" (1 Timothy 4:12).

Young children may feel powerless to communicate their growing faith. Use the Key Verse to show them that their words, faith, and actions are important to God. Remind them that God promises to always stay with them, wherever they go and whatever they face.

THE LION AND THE BEAR 📖

(up to 10 minutes)

Hang three sheets of newsprint on a classroom wall. On the first sheet of newsprint, write, "The Lord who helped me with _____ will help me with _____."

Gather the children on the floor and ask:

● **What kinds of hard situations has God helped you with in the past?** (God helped me when I was sick; God helped me with my spelling test; God helped my family when my dad lost his job; God helped my family when my grandma died.)

Write children's answers on the second sheet of newsprint. Ask:

● **What kinds of hard situations do you face now?** (I'm scared that my parents will get a divorce; I have to sing a solo at school; I need help learning how to read well.)

Write children's answers on the third sheet of newsprint.

Form pairs. Say: **David knew that God would help him fight Goliath because God had already helped him fight a lion and a bear.** Read **1 Samuel 17:37 aloud. We can know that God will help us with hard things we face now and in the future because God has helped us with hard situations in the past.**

With your partner, think of a poem that shows how God will help you. Pick one item from the list of things that God has already helped us with to put in the first blank. Pick another item from the list of things that we need help with to put in the second blank. Your poem doesn't have to rhyme.

Give children a minute to make up poems. Then have volunteers share their poems with the rest of the class.

Say: **It's good to remember what God has already done for us because it helps us have faith that no matter what we face in the future, ✦ God can help us do things that seem impossible.**

★ THE POINT

We believe that Christian education extends beyond the classroom into the home. Photocopy the "Growing Together" handout (p. 82) for this week, and send it home with your children. Encourage children and parents to use the handout to plan meaningful activities on this week's topic. Follow up the "Growing Together" activities next week by asking children what their families did together.

GROWING TOGETHER

# CLOSING

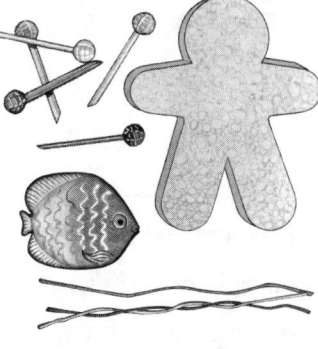

GIANT SLAYERS
(up to 10 minutes)

Ask:

● **What did you learn today?** (I learned that God gives me strength; I learned that God is always with me; I learned that God can help me do things that seem impossible.)

Stick *glitter pins* in the feet of the *foam person* to create a base so the *foam person* can stand up. Make a G for Goliath from one or two *Wikki Stix,* and pin the letter to the *foam person's* chest.

Have the children sit in a circle. Stand the *foam person* in the middle of the circle. Say: **Let's pretend that this is Goliath, the giant. Goliath is going to represent the biggest challenge you're facing right now, the task that seems the most impossible. Take a minute to think of what's hardest for you. You don't have to tell anyone.**

Give the children a few seconds to think of something. Then say: ✦ **God can help us do things that seem impossible, so we're going to defeat this giant. God is so strong that defeating the biggest giant is a cinch. To remind us of God's strength, we're going to knock over this strong giant with a tiny puff of air from the *squirty fish.***

**THE POINT** ★

When it's your turn, ask God to help you face your tough challenge, then puff some air from the *squirty fish* at the giant's head. The rest of us will say, "God will help you do it." Then set up the giant again, and give the fish to the next person in the circle.

Go around the circle, and have each child puff the giant over with the *squirty fish.* Have the class say, "God will help you do it" for each child. When everyone's had a turn, retrieve the *squirty fish* and *foam person,* then pray: **Thank you, God, for helping us do things that seem impossible. We know that you're strong enough to help us face anything. Please be with us this week as we serve you. In Jesus' name, amen.**

DAVID 6:

God can help us do things that seem impossible.

KEY VERSE

"Don't let anyone look down on you because you are young, but set an example for the believers in speech, in life, in love, in faith and in purity" (1 Timothy 4:12).

GROWING TOGETHER

I·N T·O·U·C·H

Today your child learned that God has amazing power and that God gives us strength to face tough challenges just as God gave David the strength to fight Goliath. The children learned that God is always with us and will always give us the help we need. Use these activities at home to teach your child about strength that comes from God.

STRONG FAITH

Show your child that strong faith comes from watching and remembering what God has done. Recall times God helped your family, and write them down on a sheet of paper. Each time you write something, fold the paper in half. After five or six folds, have each family member try to rip through the paper. It is almost impossible. Explain that just as the paper is strengthened by layering, faith is strengthened each time we see God work in our lives.

HEROES FOR GOD

Help your child develop his or her own hero costume using old clothes and household props. Read Ephesians 6:10-18 for ideas. Add pieces to the costume to represent special talents God has given to your child. For example, you might create a large music note out of fabric to glue onto your child's shirt if he or she likes to sing to God. Remind your child that a true hero's strength comes from God.

MARSHMALLOW PEOPLE

Make your own marshmallows. Mix a large package of flavored gelatin with 1½ cups boiling water in a large bowl. Stir until dissolved. Add ½ cup white corn syrup, and stir well. Refrigerate until mixture starts to thicken. Then beat with an electric mixer until fluffy. Pour the mixture into a small baking pan, and let set until firm. Cut into 25 cubes, and roll each cube in powdered sugar. Make marshmallow people by connecting the marshmallow cubes with toothpicks or uncooked spaghetti. Talk about how God strengthens us just as the toothpicks strengthen the marshmallow people. Then enjoy eating the marshmallows together.

GOD'S AMAZING WORLD

Take a walk, and collect pine cones. Or buy several at a craft store. Soak one in water for a minute. Its scales will close. Set it in a warm windowsill. Come back several hours later or the next day, and the scales will be open. The pine cone protects its seeds from being scattered before the ground is ready. When the ground is warm, the cone opens up and releases the seeds. Talk about the protection that God gives people. What kind of protection does God give you and your family that helps you face tough times? Put the pine cones in a pretty bowl, and use them as a centerpiece to remind your family of God's strength and protection.

A·L·W·A·Y·S

K·I·N·D

THE POINT
God helps us be kind, even when people are mean to us.

THE BIBLE BASIS:
1 Samuel 24:1-22. David spares Saul's life.

David faced a tough decision when he caught Saul in an unprotected moment. David finally had an opportunity to give the king what he deserved for terrorizing his life. David must have longed for the satisfaction that revenge would have given, especially since David's men were urging him strongly that revenge was what God wanted. Yet David did nothing more than cut off a corner of Saul's robe. Then he convinced his men to leave Saul unharmed and lamented his decision to cut Saul's robe. He said, "Saul is the Lord's appointed king. I should not do anything against him."

First- and second-graders have opportunities every day to take advantage of others and to seek revenge against those who have wronged them. Sometimes that impulse for a payback is almost impossible to curb. Your students will understand David's struggle to be kind to a bully. Use this example to teach them what it means to turn the other cheek and to let God be the judge of others' actions.

Other Scriptures used in this lesson are **Proverbs 15:1; Hosea 11:4;** and **Ephesians 4:32.**

KEY VERSE
for Lessons 5–8

"Don't let anyone look down on you because you are young, but set an example for the believers in speech, in life, in love, in faith and in purity"
(1 Timothy 4:12).

GETTING THE POINT

Children will

- discover they can act with kindness instead of getting even,
- learn that kindness shows love for others and love for God, and
- learn strategies for responding with kindness in the toughest situations.

Before the lesson, collect the items from the Learning Lab for the activities you plan to use. Refer to the pictures in the margin to see what each item looks like.

THIS LESSON AT A GLANCE

SECTION	MINUTES	WHAT CHILDREN WILL DO	LEARNING LAB SUPPLIES	CLASSROOM SUPPLIES
WELCOME TIME	up to 5	**Welcome!**—Receive a warm welcome from the teacher and make name tags.		"Outside-Inside Name Tags" (p. 73), scissors, markers, tape or safety pins
ATTENTION GRABBER	up to 10	**Old Monkey**—Play a game in which they give a game piece to others in order to win the game and talk about how they react when others treat them in ways they don't like.	Glitter pins, plastic monkeys	
BIBLE EXPLORATION & APPLICATION	up to 10	**The Bully King**—Participate in the story of David's sparing Saul's life based on 1 Samuel 24:1-22.	Cassette: "The Bully King"	Bible, cassette player
	up to 10	**Kindness Songs**—Sing "This Is My Commandment," listen to "Jesus Loves Me," read Ephesians 4:32, and learn that they can show kindness to others because God shows kindness to them.	"Lyrics Poster," cassette: "This Is My Commandment," "Jesus Loves Me"	Bible, cassette player
	up to 15	**Kindness Rope**—Read in Hosea 11:4 about God's kindness to people and make a rope of kind actions that will show God's love to others.	Wikki Stix	Bible
CLOSING	up to 10	**Gentle Answers**—Read Proverbs 15:1 and practice giving gentle answers in response to mean actions.	Paper globe	Bible

Remember to make photocopies of the "Growing Together" handout (p. 91) to send home with your children. "Growing Together" is a valuable tool for helping first- and second-graders talk with their parents about what they're learning in class.

ELCOME TIME

WELCOME!
(up to 5 minutes)

- Greet each child individually with an enthusiastic smile.
- Thank each child for coming to class today.
- As children arrive, ask them about last week's "Growing Together" discussion. Use questions such as "How did God's power help you with a hard task last week?" and "Just as the pine cone protected its seeds in the water, how does God protect you?"
- Say: **Today we're going to learn that** ✦ **God helps us be kind, even when people are mean to us.**
- Hand out the name tags children made during Lesson 5, and help children attach the name tags to their clothing. If some of the name tags were damaged, or if children weren't in class that week, have them make new name tags using the photocopiable handout on page 73.
- Tell children that the attention-getting signal you'll use during this lesson is clapping your hands three times. Ask children to respond by clapping their hands three times as they stop talking and focus their attention on you. Rehearse the signal with the children, telling them to respond quickly so you have plenty of time for all the fun activities planned for this lesson.

THE POINT

TTENTION GRABBER

OLD MONKEY
(up to 10 minutes)

LEARNING LAB

Give each child three different-colored *glitter pins*. Give three or four of the children a *plastic monkey* also. No more than one-fourth of the children should have monkeys.

Say: **In this game, the object is to get three pins of the same color and to not have a monkey. To play the game, ask anyone for a pin that's a color you want. For example, if I decide I want to try to get**

three green pins, I'll ask everyone for a green pin. If the people I ask have one, they must give it to me. If they don't, I'll find someone else to ask. If they have a monkey, they can give that to me instead. It doesn't matter what color the monkey is. Once you have three pins that are the same color and you don't have any monkeys, sit down along the edge of the wall and wait for the game to be over.

Play the game for a few minutes or until there are several children sitting by the wall. Call time by blowing the *balloon squawker.* Collect the *glitter pins* and *plastic monkeys,* then have children gather on the floor. Ask:

● **What was it like when you gave a monkey away?** (I was thankful that I didn't have it any more; I felt glad.)

● **What was it like when you got a monkey?** (Bad, because then I had to get rid of it; I was mad that my friend gave me the monkey.)

● **In real life, how do you feel when someone does something to you that you don't like?** (Mad; sad; like that person doesn't like me.)

● **Do you ever want to get back at people who do things to you that you don't like? Why or why not?** (Yes, because they deserve it; no, because it's not nice.)

Say: **It hurts when people do things to us we don't like. It can make us mad and make us want to get even. But ✹ God helps us be kind, even when people are mean to us. Today we're going to hear about a person who had mean things done to him. This person had the perfect chance to get even with the man who did all the mean things. We're going to find out what happened.**

Teacher Tip

It's important to say The Point just as it's written in each activity. Repeating The Point over and over will help children remember it and apply it to their lives.

★ THE POINT

BIBLE EXPLORATION & APPLICATION

THE BULLY KING 📖

(up to 10 minutes)

LEARNING LAB

Cue the *cassette tape* to "The Bully King." Open your Bible to **1 Samuel 24:1-22,** and show the passage to the children. Say: **This Bible story is about a king who was a bully. So each time you hear King Saul say something evil, laugh an evil, wicked laugh such as "Heh-heh-heh." The story is also about a man who was strong and kind. So whenever you hear the word "David," say, "Strong and kind." Let's practice. Evil King Saul.** Pause for children to say, "Heh-heh-heh." **David.** Pause for children to say, "Strong and kind."

Say: **The story's on our *cassette tape.* You'll have to listen carefully and be ready to chime in with your part, because the voice on the tape won't wait long for you to say your part. Ready? Here we go.**

Start the tape, and say "heh-heh-heh" and "strong and kind" along with the children. When the story ends, stop the cassette player, and ask:

● **Why was Saul so mean to David?** (Because people liked David better; because David did things better than Saul did.)

● **Why didn't David get even with Saul when he had the chance?** (Because David was strong and kind; because he knew God didn't want him to.)

● **Do you think it was easy for David to be kind to Saul? Why or why not?** (Yes, because he was a hero; no, because Saul was so mean.)

● **Have you ever been treated as David was treated? Tell me about it. What did you do?** (Yes, there's a bully on my street who likes to punch me—I turned the other cheek, but he hit that one, too; yes, I prayed for a teacher who didn't like me, and she started treating me better.)

Say: **Saul was jealous of David because all the people in Israel thought David was a bigger hero than Saul was. But David didn't respond to Saul's meanness with more meanness. David was kind to Saul. He kept his men from killing Saul, and he promised to be kind to Saul's entire family. David's actions pleased God. ✯ God helps us be kind, even when people are mean to us. We can be kind just as David was kind.**

KINDNESS SONGS 📖

(up to 10 minutes)

Cue the *cassette tape* to "This Is My Commandment." Take down the Time-Stuffer poster, and turn it over to the "Lyrics Poster" side. Choose a volunteer to hold the poster. Choose another volunteer to point to the words as you sing them.

Say: **God commands us to love each other. ✯ He wants us to be kind, even when people are mean to us. Let's sing a song to remind us to be kind to others.**

Sing the song with the children. Ask:

● **How does being loving and kind give us joy?** (Because we're doing what God wants; because it makes others feel good about us.)

● **Do you think David's acts of kindness toward Saul made David joyful? Explain.** (Yes, because he knew he was doing what God wanted; maybe not, because he had to keep hiding from the king.)

● **How can you show kindness to people who aren't always nice to you?** (I can play with them; I can forgive them; I can smile at them.)

Say: **I'm going to play a song that's probably very familiar to you. But I'd like you to listen to the words carefully, as if you were hearing them for the first time. Then I'm going to ask you to tell a partner what you learned from this song about how God shows kindness to us.**

Play "Jesus Loves Me" on the *cassette tape.* Then have children form pairs, and allow a minute for partners to share.

BIBLE INSIGHT

Saul's bitter pursuit of David may have led to Saul's eventual defeat by the Philistines. While he chased David, Saul's government suffered. The economies of the separate tribes dwindled, and the training of a large army was neglected. Also, little attention was paid to the construction of educational and spiritual institutions.

THE POINT ★

LEARNING LAB

THE POINT ★

LEARNING LAB

Ask:

● **What did you learn from this song about the kindness that God shows us?** (God forgives us when we sin; God wants us to belong to him.)

Say: **God loves us even though we sometimes do things that make him sad. Listen to what the Bible says about how God wants us to share kindness and forgiveness with others.** Read **Ephesians 4:32** aloud. **We can be kind and forgiving to others no matter what they've done to us, because God is kind and forgiving to us. Turn to your partner again. Without naming names, tell your partner about someone who hasn't always been kind to you, then tell one way you can show kindness to that person.**

Allow a minute or two for partners to share. Then clap your hands three times to get children's attention. Wait for them to respond, then invite partners to share ideas from their discussions.

Then say: **Let's pray about being kind in the situations you've just discussed with your partners. Dear Lord, it's not always easy to be kind to people who are mean to us. But you gave David strength to be kind, and we believe you can help us be kind, too. Please help us be kind and willing to forgive this week, just the way you've forgiven us. In Jesus' name, amen.**

KINDNESS ROPE 📖

(up to 15 minutes)

Say: **Let's find out what happens when we're kind to people who are mean to us. Listen to this Bible verse, and be ready to tell me who was kind.** Read **Hosea 11:4.** Ask:

● **Who was kind?** (God.)

● **What did God do?** (God led people with kindness.)

Say: **God led the people to him with kindness because they had wandered away from him. They were doing things that made God sad. When God was kind to them, they came back. Let's make our own rope of kindness right now.**

Have children stand in a circle. Gather all of the *Wikki-Stix* pieces from the Learning Lab. Unbend them, and distribute them to the children. Say: **One by one you'll take your *Wikki Stix* and attach it to the *Wikki Stix* of the person on your right. As you attach it, tell that person one way he or she can show God's love and kindness to people who are mean. For example, you might say, "You can encourage someone who's put you down" or "You can smile and be friendly to someone who's rude." As we go around the circle, our *Wikki Stix* will form a rope of kindness.**

Be ready to help children who have trouble thinking of ideas or who have trouble twisting their *Wikki Stix* together. Ask:

● **How do you feel when you're kind to people who have been mean to you?** (Good; I feel like God is happy with me.)

● **What do you think people who are mean to you will do when you**

treat them kindly? (They'll be surprised; they might be nicer to me.)

Say: ✦ **God helps us be kind, even when people are mean to us. When we treat mean people with kindness, it shows them how God will treat them—it shows them that God loves them. God is always willing to gently lead people back to him.**

Have children stand and hold the kindness rope as you gently lead them around the room. Then ask:

● **What was it like to be led with the kindness rope?** (I had to be careful not to break the rope; I wanted to make it easy for the leader.)

Say: **When we treat others with kindness, we lead them to God. We may not see a big change right away, but we know that our acts of kindness help them see God's love.**

We believe that Christian education extends beyond the classroom into the home. *GROWING TOGETHER* Photocopy the "Growing Together" handout (p. 91) for this week, and send it home with your children. Encourage children and parents to use the handout to plan meaningful activities on this week's topic. Follow up the "Growing Together" activities next week by asking children what their families did together.

CLOSING

GENTLE ANSWERS 📖

(up to 10 minutes)

Ask:

● **What did you learn today?** (I learned that I should be kind; I learned to be nice to my enemies; I learned that God will help me be kind, even when others are mean.)

Have the children sit on the floor. Inflate the *paper globe,* and say: **Let's pretend this is a person who's been mean to us. I blew him up with all of the mean acts that he's done. Let's practice one thing we can do to treat others with kindness when they're mean to us. Listen to this Bible verse to discover what we can do.** Read **Proverbs 15:1.** Ask:

● **What can we do when someone does angry, mean things to us?** (We can be gentle; we can say kind things.)

LEARNING LAB

Bring a hand-held hair dryer and an extension cord to class, and have the children try to keep the globe afloat by turning the dryer on the cool setting at low speed.

Say: **Let's have fun giving gentle answers to this anger-filled person. We'll pretend that our puffs of breath are kind, gentle answers. Let's see if our gentle answers can keep the** *paper globe* **in the air.**

When every child has had a chance to blow on the *paper globe,* put it away, then ask:

● **Was it easy to turn away anger with your gentle answers? Why or why not?** (No, it was hard because the globe kept getting away from me; no, it took a lot of breath; I thought it was fun.)

● **What makes it hard in real life to be gentle to someone who's been mean?** (It's hard, because I feel bad when others are mean and I don't want to be nice; it's hard, because it hurts when they're mean.)

Say: **Sometimes it takes a lot of work to be gentle and kind when others are mean to us, but that's what God helps us do.** Ask:

● **What gentle things can you say to people who have been mean to you?** (I can say that I forgive them; I can say that I want to be their friend anyway; I can ask them to come over and play with me.)

Say: **Those are great ideas! It may be hard, but** ✯ **God helps us be kind, even when people are mean to us. He loves us, cares for us, and helps us be kind.**

DAVID 7:

God helps us be kind, even when people are mean to us.

KEY VERSE

"Don't let anyone look down on you because you are young, but set an example for the believers in speech, in life, in love, in faith and in purity" (1 Timothy 4:12).

GROWING TOGETHER

I·N T·O·U·C·H

Today your child learned that God helps us be kind to others no matter what they've done to us. Our kindness is an example of the love, kindness, and forgiveness that God gives to us. Use these activities at home to teach your child to be kind to others.

BALL SLAMS

Draw a smiley face on a tennis ball. Hit or throw the tennis ball against an outdoor wall. Tell your child that no matter how many times a person treats us with meanness, we should always bounce back with kindness. Each time you hit the ball, think of a mean act. Each time the ball bounces back, think of a kind response.

GOLDEN ACTS

Teach your child the golden rule from Matthew 7:12a: "Do to others what you would have them do to you." Then give your child a stack of index cards, and have him or her draw pictures of kind things to do for others. Also draw pictures of kind actions your child enjoys receiving. Spray paint a container with gold paint, and keep the cards inside it. Have your child choose at least one card per week and do that kind action for a friend or family member.

THUMB-PRINT COOKIES

Heat oven to 350°. Mix ¼ cup packed brown sugar, ½ cup shortening, ½ teaspoon vanilla, and 1 egg yolk. Stir in 1 cup flour. Shape the dough into 1-inch balls. Press your thumb deeply into each ball of dough, and talk about how mean actions can make us feel like we've been punched. Bake the cookies about 10 minutes or until light brown. Remove them

from the cookie sheet, and fill the thumb print with your favorite jelly. Talk about filling up the hole caused by meanness with sweet kindness.

ATTRACTIVE KINDNESS

Lay out a sheet of wax paper and a toothpick. Dribble several drops of water on the wax paper, and have your child move them around the paper with the toothpick. See how close your child can get two water drops to each other before they "jump" together and form one larger water drop. Talk about how kindness makes us attractive to others and how others want to be with people who are kind.

B·E
W·I·S·E

THE POINT
God wants us
to act wisely.

THE BIBLE BASIS: 📖
1 Samuel 25:1-35. Abigail brings food to David.

When Nabal denied hospitality to David and his men, David was furious. He immediately set his mind on vengeance. But Nabal's wife, Abigail, used her intellect and her calm, gentle wisdom to defuse the situation before any blood was shed. Abigail convinced David that he would regret carrying out his impulsive plan of vengeance even though Nabal deserved to be punished. David listened to Abigail and took time to think, instead of acting rashly.

First- and second-graders (along with many adults!) need to learn to step back and think before they act. When children face frustrating or negative situations, they often do the first thing that comes to mind and

create more trouble for themselves than they had before. We can share with children the importance of stopping to ask, "What would God want me to do?" Use this lesson to help children ask for and rely on God's wisdom.

Other Scriptures used in this lesson are **Proverbs 1:7; Proverbs 19:2; Song of Songs 2:4;** and **Hebrews 5:13-14.**

KEY VERSE
for Lessons 5–8

"Don't let anyone look down on you because you are young, but set an example for the believers in speech, in life, in love, in faith and in purity"
(1 Timothy 4:12).

GETTING THE POINT

Children will

- learn that wisdom begins with respect for God,
- discover that God gives wisdom when they ask for it, and
- develop a plan to wait on wisdom.

Before the lesson, collect the items from the Learning Lab for the activities you plan to use. Refer to the pictures in the margin to see what each item looks like.

THIS LESSON AT A GLANCE

SECTION	MINUTES	WHAT CHILDREN WILL DO	LEARNING LAB SUPPLIES	CLASSROOM SUPPLIES
WELCOME TIME	up to 5	**Welcome!**—Receive a warm welcome from the teacher and make name tags.		"Outside-Inside Name Tags" (p. 73), scissors, markers, tape or safety pins
ATTENTION GRABBER	up to 10	**Puzzle Scramble**—Put a puzzle together and learn that sometimes they need help to figure out tough problems.	Crayon car puzzle	
BIBLE EXPLORATION & APPLICATION	up to 10	**Wise Advice**—Act out the story of David, Nabal, and Abigail from 1 Samuel and learn about the wise advice that David received from Abigail.	Plastic monkeys	Bible
	up to 10	**Quick to Move**—Play a game and learn from Proverbs 1:7 that they can get into trouble if they act too quickly.		Bible
	up to 15	**The Banqueting Table**—Hear Song of Songs 2:4 and eat a snack from "God's banqueting table" to learn that God's wisdom is always available. Then discover from Hebrews 5:13-14 the difference between milk and solid food.		Bible, small paper cups, milk, treat
CLOSING	up to 10	**W.O.W.**—Hear Proverbs 19:2; make reminders that will help them wait, think, and pray before they act; and pray for God's wisdom.	Crayon car puzzle	Bible, paper, markers, "W.O.W." photocopies

Remember to make photocopies of the "Growing Together" handout (p. 102) to send home with your children. "Growing Together" is a valuable tool for helping first- and second-graders talk with their parents about what they're learning in class.

T·H·E L·E·S·S·O·N

WELCOME TIME

WELCOME!
(up to 5 minutes)

- Greet each child individually with an enthusiastic smile.
- Thank each child for coming to class today.
- As children arrive, ask them about last week's "Growing Together" discussion. Use questions such as "How did your smiley-face tennis ball remind you to bounce back with kindness?" and "When did God help you show kindness last week?"
- Say: **Today we're going to learn that ★ God wants us to act wisely.**

THE POINT ★

- Hand out the name tags children made during Lesson 5, and help children attach the name tags to their clothing. If some of the name tags were damaged, or if children weren't in class that week, have them make new name tags using the photocopiable handout on page 73.
- Tell children that the attention-getting signal you'll use during this lesson is clapping your hands three times. Ask children to respond by clapping their hands three times as they stop talking and focus their attention on you. Rehearse the signal with the children, telling them to respond quickly so you have plenty of time for all the fun activities planned for this lesson.

MODULE REVIEW

Use the casual interaction at the beginning of class to ask the children the following module-review questions:

- **Why doesn't God judge us by the way we look?**
- **When did God help you do something that seemed impossible?**
- **Have you been kind lately to someone who was mean to you? What happened?**
- **What's your favorite thing we've learned during the past few weeks? Why?**

ATTENTION GRABBER

PUZZLE SCRAMBLE

(up to 10 minutes)

Before class, take the *crayon car puzzle* apart. It's easiest if you pull the wheels off first.

As children arrive, give each one a puzzle piece. If you have more than eight students in your class, form eight groups. It's fine if the groups aren't the same size.

Once all the puzzle pieces are distributed, say: **Work together to put these pieces together.** Give children about a minute to work on the puzzle without any direction. Then, if they need help, give hints such as "It's a car" or "All the pieces fit on the black piece with the posts" or "Try putting the wheels on first."

When children have finished putting the puzzle together, say: **Great job! It took good thinking and teamwork to get this puzzle back together.** Ask:

● **Was this puzzle easy to figure out? Explain.** (Yes, I've seen puzzles like this before; yes, I'm good at puzzles; no, I didn't know what it was supposed to be; no, it was hard to work with others.)

● **What kinds of things are hard for you to figure out in real life?** (Math; riding a bicycle; puzzles; spelling.)

● **What do you do when you come across something that's hard to figure out?** (I try hard; I ask God to help; I ask my parents to help; I ask my big sister to help.)

Set the *crayon car puzzle* aside for use in a later activity.

Say: **When we come across hard things, we need to ask for help. Today we're going to learn about a time David was helped in a tough situation. We'll learn that ✦ God wants us to act wisely. Sometimes other people can help us do that.**

> ### Teacher Tip
> It's important to say The Point just as it's written in each activity. Repeating The Point over and over will help children remember it and apply it to their lives.

★ THE POINT

B IBLE EXPLORATION & APPLICATION

WISE ADVICE 📖

(up to 10 minutes)

Form groups of three. Give a green, purple, and orange *plastic monkey* to each group. Have each group decide who gets the monkey of each color.

Open your Bible to **1 Samuel 25:1-35** and show the passage to the children. Say: **Our story today is from 1 Samuel. It's about three people—David, Nabal, and Abigail. If you have an orange monkey, you're David; if you have a purple monkey, you're Nabal; and, if you have a green monkey, you're Abigail. Listen for your part in the story, and be ready to follow my actions. Here we go.**

David was in the desert with his men. They'd been hiding from Saul's army, so they didn't have very much food. They were tired from running away from Saul, and they were hungry, too.

There was a man named Nabal who lived in the desert. Nabal was rich—he had many sheep and goats and lots of money. Have the Nabals pretend to count money. **His wife was named Abigail, and she was wise and beautiful.** Have the Abigails point to their heads then fan their hands around their faces. **But Nabal was cruel and mean.** Have the Nabals growl.

While David was in the desert, he heard that Nabal was cutting the wool off of his sheep. David gathered 10 of his men and sent them to Nabal. Have the Davids hold up 10 fingers then point. **David said, "When you meet Nabal, say, 'May you and your family have good health.' Then remind Nabal that we have made sure that his shepherds and his sheep were safe. And even though we've been hungry, we haven't stolen any sheep to eat. Tell Nabal to be kind to you. See if he has any food or supplies that he can give us."**

When David's men gave the message to Nabal, Nabal insulted them. Have the Nabals growl. **He said, "I don't even know this man you call David. Are you sure that you aren't slaves who've run away from your masters? I have food for my own workers, but I don't give it to people I don't know."**

The men went back and told David what Nabal had said to them. David was furious. Have the Davids jump up and down and put their hands on their hips. **He said, "All of our kindnesses were useless. I took care of Nabal in the desert. I was good to him, and he has paid me back with evil." David commanded, "Put on your swords. We'll pay Nabal back for his unkindness to us." Four hundred of David's men put on their swords and got ready for battle.** Have the Davids pretend to buckle swords around their waists.

Abigail found out that her husband, Nabal, had been mean to David's men. A servant told her, "David's men were very good to us. They protected us while we took care of the sheep, and they never took any of our sheep to eat. And now because Nabal refused to help them, they're coming to attack us and get even." Have the Abigails press their hands to their cheeks and say, "Oh, no!"

Abigail knew there was no time to waste. She hurried to gather 200 loaves of bread, two leather bags of wine, five cooked sheep, a bushel of grain, 100 raisin cakes, and 200 fig cakes. Have the Abigails pretend to gather a lot of food. **She loaded all of the supplies on donkeys and told her servants to take them to David's men.** Have the Abigails pretend to load donkeys with a lot of food.

Teacher Tip

If you don't have enough monkeys to go around, use orange, blue, and pink *glitter pins*. Have kids with orange glitter pins play David, kids with blue glitter pins play Nabal, and kids with pink *glitter pins* play Abigail.

BIBLE INSIGHT

David wasn't unreasonable to expect a favor from Nabal. David had provided a valuable service by protecting Nabal's flocks in the desert. Shepherds faced the same dangers the sheep faced—harsh weather; thieves; and the threat of wolves, bears, lions, and panthers. Without David's help, Nabal might never have had the 3,000 sheep the Bible mentions.

Abigail went with the servants and met with David. When she saw David, she quickly got off her donkey. She bowed face down on the ground in front of him and said, "It's all my fault. Please listen to what I say. Nabal has been very foolish. Please forgive the wrong that's been done to you. I have brought a gift for you." Have the Abigails kneel down as if begging David.

"I'm so sorry that we have wronged you, because your family is blessed," Abigail continued. "I pray that God keeps you safe always. God will keep all of his promises to you. He'll make you a great king. You'll be so glad on that day that you didn't kill innocent people and punish them. Please remember this and me when God brings success to you." Have the Abigails fold their hands and plead.

David listened to what Abigail said and knew she was right. Have the Davids rub their chins and nod their heads. David said, "Praise God for sending you to me. You are blessed with great wisdom. You have kept me from punishing people today."

Then David accepted the food gifts that Abigail had brought. Have the Abigails hold out food. And he said to her, "Go home in peace. I have heard your wise words, and I'll do as you ask."

Have children give themselves a round of applause for their participation in the story. Return the *plastic monkeys* to the Learning Lab, then ask:

● **How was Nabal unwise?** (If he'd given supplies to David, David wouldn't have wanted to attack him; he was mean to David's men.)

● **How was Abigail wise?** (She kept the men from fighting; she took food to David's men.)

● **How was David unwise?** (He forgot to be kind to people who are mean; he was ready to fight.)

● **How was David wise?** (He listened to Abigail; he didn't fight Nabal.)

THE POINT

Say: **Everybody acts unwisely some of the time even though ✦ God wants us to act wisely all of the time. David had just been kind to Saul, who wanted to kill him. But then he was ready to attack Nabal for being mean. But Abigail was very wise. She gave David good advice, and he listened to it. David almost did something unwise because he decided too quickly. Let's find out more about making decisions too quickly.**

QUICK TO MOVE 📖

(up to 10 minutes)

This game works best in a large room or outside. If you play it in your class-room, move the furniture against the walls to create an open space. Have the children line up along one wall on their hands and knees.

Say: **This game is played like Moving Statues, except that instead of running toward the other side of the room, you'll crawl as fast as you can. Be** ready to stop, though, because I can turn around and say "gotcha" at any time. Then you have to be as still as a statue. If you move even a tiny bit, I'll point to you, and you'll have to go back to the beginning.

Face the wall and say "go." Then quickly turn and say "gotcha!" Send any children you catch moving back to the starting line. Play the game until everyone reaches the finish line. Then ask:

● **Was it easy to become as still as a statue when you were moving so fast? Why or why not?** (Yes, I was pretty good at it; no, because I never knew when you would turn around.)

Say: **Just as it was hard to stop in our game, sometimes it's hard to control our actions. Listen to what the Bible says about being in control of our actions.** Read **Proverbs 1:7** aloud. **The Bible tells us that part of being wise is to respect God. Another part of being wise is to be in control. Let's slow down this game so we can be in better control of our actions.**

Choose a volunteer to be the caller. Have the children line up again on the opposite side of the room. Play the game again, but this time have children crawl in slow motion so they can stop when they see the caller start to turn around. When everyone has reached the finish line, gather the children and ask:

● **Was it easier or harder to play the game like this? Explain.** (It was easier, because I could see the caller start to turn; it was harder, because it was so slow that I got impatient to get to the end.)

● **When is it better to go slowly in real life?** (When you might hurt yourself if you go too fast; when you might hurt someone else; when you're mad.)

Say: ✦ **God wants us to act wisely so we don't get ourselves into trouble. Sometimes that means taking our time. In our game, not so many of you got caught when you went slowly. Real life is the same way—when we make slow, careful decisions, we're less likely to get in trouble. David almost hurt a lot of people because he decided to get revenge instead of being wise. Abigail convinced David to slow down and think about his actions. Abigail acted with God's wisdom. Let's find out more about the wisdom that God wants to give to us.**

THE POINT ★

THE BANQUETING TABLE 📖

(up to 15 minutes)

Say: **You all worked hard in that race. I bet you're hungry. Gather around the table because I have a banquet for you. But first, listen to what the Bible says about a banquet.** Read **Song of Songs 2:4** aloud. **God is going to bring us to a banqueting table. Let's get it ready.**

Help the children set out a table and put chairs around it. When the children are sitting around the table, bring out small paper cups, and pour milk into them. Say: **Enjoy your banquet!** If the children ask about the lack of food, say: **But the milk is your banquet. Milk has all the vitamins you need to**

"Don't let anyone look down on you because you are young, but set an example for the believers in speech, in life, in love, in faith and in purity" (1 Timothy 4:12).

Wisdom is a lifelong pursuit that can begin in childhood. Remind children that God called David at an early age. Use this Key Verse to emphasize to children that God values them.

 **THE POINT**

grow strong and healthy. **Drink up!** After a few moments, ask:

● **Don't you like your banquet? Explain.** (No, I don't like milk; yes, milk is good; no, I wanted real food.)

Say: **Milk is a little bit like God's wisdom. When we drink milk we get strong, and when we listen to God's wisdom and take it inside our hearts, we get wise. The Bible says to drink up the milk of God's wisdom and teaching. But the Bible says something else about milk.** Read **Hebrews 5:13-14** aloud. **None of you is a baby anymore. You eat solid food. And you're ready to learn more about the Bible and the solid food of God's wisdom, too.**

Pass out a treat that goes well with milk, such as doughnut holes or cookies. While the children are eating, ask:

● **What kinds of actions does God consider to be wise?** (Things that help others; obeying my parents; following the rules that are in the Bible; doing things that keep me safe.)

● **What situations do you face in which you need God's wisdom?** (I don't know what to do about my sister—she's always mean to me; I don't know how to be nice to my next-door neighbor; I need help learning how to spell and sound out words.)

Say: **When you need wisdom from God, all you have to do is come to God's banqueting table. God has wisdom ready for you—you can find it in his Word. Take in the good things you find in the Bible as eagerly as you eat cookies and milk.** ✦ **God wants us to act wisely, and by "feasting" on God's Word, each of you will become wiser.**

Help the children clean up the cups from the snack.

We believe that Christian education extends beyond the classroom into the home. **GROWING TOGETHER** Photocopy the "Growing Together" handout (p. 102) for this week, and send it home with your children. Encourage children and parents to use the handout to plan meaningful activities on this week's topic. Follow up the "Growing Together" activities next week by asking children what their families did together.

 # CLOSING

W.O.W. 📖

(up to 10 minutes)

Draw a stop sign on a piece of paper, and write "W.O.W." on it. Photocopy the drawing for each child. Ask:

● **What did you learn today?** (I learned that God wants to make me wise; I learned that being wise means not making decisions quickly.)

Say: **Listen to what the Bible says about acting quickly.** Read **Proverbs 19:2** aloud. **An example of being unwise and acting too quickly is running out into the street to get a ball without looking for traffic first.** Ask:

● **Have you ever done something quickly and then found out it was unwise? Tell me about it.** (Yes, once I got mad at my friend for doing something, and then I found out she didn't do it; yes, once I started to run down the stairs too quickly and fell all the way down.)

Say: **Sometimes the wisest thing we can do is to stop and think about what we're going to do before we do it. Let's make something that will remind us to think before we act.**

Give each child a "W.O.W." drawing. Say: **"W.O.W." stands for "Wait On Wisdom." Draw a picture of yourself stopping to think about what you'll do before you do it.**

Let children use the pieces of the *crayon car puzzle* to draw their pictures. Set out extra crayons if you have more than seven students. While the children are working, ask about the situations they're drawing. Ask:

● **What kind of trouble could you get into if you acted too quickly?** (I could get hurt; I could mess up a friendship; I could cause an accident.)

● **How can you act wisely?** (Wait until I know all the facts; wait until I'm not mad anymore; figure out the answer carefully; look both ways before I run out into the street.)

Say: ⭐ **God wants us to act wisely. We can be wise by stopping to think about our actions. When we stop to think, we can ask God to give us wisdom, and God promises to give it to us. Let's ask God for wisdom right now.**

 **THE POINT** ⭐

Pray: **God, thank you for being ready to give us wisdom when we need it. We ask for your help and wisdom in the situations we face every day. Help us to wait on your wisdom instead of acting too quickly. In Jesus' name, amen.**

Return the *crayon car puzzle* to the Learning Lab.

DAVID 8:

God wants us to act wisely.

KEY VERSE

"Don't let anyone look down on you because you are young, but set an example for the believers in speech, in life, in love, in faith and in purity" *(1 Timothy 4:12).*

GROWING TOGETHER

Today your child learned that God wants us to act with wisdom. The children learned that God is ready to give us all the wisdom we need to face any situation. The children also learned that they can make wise decisions when they stop to think about what they're going to do before they do it.

HOT OR COLD

Prepare three pans of water. One should be as hot as your child can comfortably tolerate. One should be very cold, and the third should be room temperature. Have your child put one hand in the hot water and one hand in the cold water. After one minute, have your child put both hands in the room-temperature water. One hand will "think" the water is cold—the other hand will "think" it's hot. Talk about how sometimes things seem different from how they really are. We need God's wisdom to help us know what's good and true.

FOREVER WISDOM

Make potpourri as a reminder that "the grass withers and the flowers fall, but the word [and wisdom] of our God stands forever" (Isaiah 40:8). Collect flowers, nuts, and twigs. Dry the flowers, and put their petals with the nuts and twigs in a pretty bowl. Sprinkle with potpourri oil, which can be found at craft stores. Put the potpourri where you'll see it often. Talk about why God's Word and wisdom will last forever.

OBSERVING WISDOM

Take a walk in your neighborhood with your child. Take along paper and a pen, and write down 15 things that you've never noticed before, such as a flowerpot or a bird's nest. Talk about how being observant can help a person be  wise. What kinds of things can you observe that will lead to wisdom? Talk with your child about looking for hidden dangers in certain courses of action and about observing others' attitudes and opinions.

RUBY COOKIES

Make these cookies to teach your child that "wisdom is more precious than rubies" (Proverbs 8:11a). Heat oven to 350°. Reserve 1 tablespoon cherry-flavored gelatin in a small bowl. Mix the rest of a small box of gelatin with 1 cup powdered sugar, 1 cup softened margarine, and 2¼ cups flour. Shape into 1-inch balls. Put them on a cookie sheet, and bake for 8 to 10 minutes. Remove before they get brown. Cool completely, then ice with this glaze: Add to the tablespoon of gelatin 3 tablespoons hot water. Let it stand for 5 minutes, then stir in 2 cups powdered sugar and 1 teaspoon vanilla.

F·R·I·E·N·D·S·H·I·P

Few things in life are as meaningful as true friends. A true friend will always be available to help you—even when you call at 2 a.m. from the other side of the country. A true friend rejoices with you in good times and offers a shoulder to cry on in bad times. A true friend will always stick up for you. And there is nothing better than sharing a hearty belly laugh with a true friend.

Unfortunately, it's not easy to cultivate lasting friendships. With the demands of family life, church activities, keeping up a home, and pursuing a career, not many people have time to enjoy the rewards of close friendships. Close friendships require time.

That's why it's important to teach children to value their relationships with others. The friends they make now might be the friends they keep for the rest of their lives. God calls us to make friends. God wants us to depend on each other, love each other, comfort each other, and rejoice with each other. These relationships pattern the kind of relationship that God wants to have with us. Help your students learn the skills of friend-making and friend-keeping, and teach them that above all else, God wants to be their friend.

FIVE LESSONS ON FRIENDSHIP

LESSON	PAGE	THE POINT	THE BIBLE BASIS
9—DEPENDABLE FRIENDS	107	Good friends can depend on each other.	1 Samuel 18:1-4
10—JOYFUL FRIENDS	117	Good friends are happy for each other.	1 Samuel 19:1-7
11—WORK IT OUT	125	Good friends work out problems with each other.	1 Samuel 20:1-23
12—COMFORT A FRIEND	135	Good friends comfort each other when they're sad.	1 Samuel 20:24-42
13—GOD IS OUR FRIEND	145	God wants to be our friend.	2 Samuel 2:1-7; 7:1-16

HE SIGNAL

During the lessons on friendship, your attention-getting signal will be clapping your hands three times. Have children respond by clapping their hands three times as they stop talking and focus their attention on you. Tell children about this signal before the lesson begins. Explain that it's important to respond to this signal quickly so the class can do as many fun activities as possible.

During the lessons, you'll be prompted when to use the signal.

HE FIDGET BUSTER

Whenever your students have too much energy to pay attention to the lesson, work the wiggles out with this relay race based on friendship.

Have children find partners and line up for a relay race with partners standing back to back. Have partners link arms and hop to the opposite side of the room and back. When the first pair completes the course, have the second pair race, and so on until everyone has taken a turn.

For the second race, have each pair get together with another pair to form a foursome. Have them race in foursomes. Then form groups of six, eight, 10, and so on until the entire class is hopping as a group.

Say: **You worked together to have great fun during this relay. That's what friendship is—working together and having fun. Now let's work together to learn more about being friends.**

> ## Teacher Tip
> If you have more than 12 students, form two teams and have them compete against each other for the first leg of the race.

HE TIME STUFFER

The Time Stuffer for the five lessons on friendship will be creating a friendship gallery. Provide sheets of newsprint and markers or crayons.

Have children draw pictures of themselves that will fill up an entire sheet of newsprint. Then have them circle the physical characteristics that will help them be good friends. For example, they could circle their mouths for giving smiles or for giving words of encouragement. They could circle their ears for always being ready to listen. Children may also write characteristics of a good friend on their sheets.

Hang the pictures under a sign that reads "We're good friends." Once children have drawn pictures of themselves, have them draw pictures of their best friends.

Any time children arrive early or finish an activity before others, encourage them to work on their pictures.

EMEMBERING GOD'S WORD

Each four- or five-week module focuses on a Key Bible Verse. The Key Verse for this module is "…live in harmony with one another; be sympathetic, love as brothers, be compassionate and humble" **(1 Peter 3:8)**.

This module's Key Verse will teach children that good friends who follow God will treat each other well. Have fun using these ideas any time during the lessons on friendship.

And look for the Key Verse Connection in the margin of each lesson. It will help you tie the module's Key Verse to The Point of the lesson.

HARMONIOUS FRIENDSHIPS

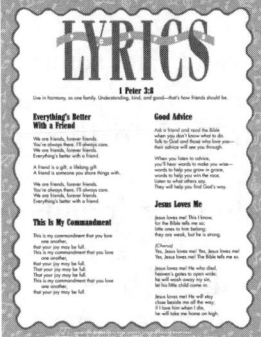

LEARNING LAB

Read **1 Peter 3:8** aloud, and have the children repeat the verse with you. Teach your children this song that paraphrases **1 Peter 3:8.** Sing it to the tune of "Row, Row, Row Your Boat." The words are also printed on the "Lyrics Poster." Hold the poster up to help children learn the words.

Live in harmony, as one family.
Understanding, kind, and good—
That's how friends should be.

If you have a helper, you might want to sing the song as a round. Ask:
● **What does it mean to live in harmony with your friends?** (It means not to fight with them; it means to be nice to them.)
● **What does it mean to live as a family?** (It means to work together; it means to do nice things for each other.)
● **How can you be understanding and kind with your friends?** (I can listen; I can let my friend choose what game to play; I can send get-well cards when my friend is sick.)

Say: **God wants everyone who believes in him to live this way. We can live as friends with all Christians.** Read **1 Peter 3:8** aloud again, and have children repeat the verse with you.

Sing the song often to help children remember the Key Verse.

LOVE AS FAMILY

LEARNING LAB

Before class, divide the *plastic monkeys* and *glitter pins* into groups of three. In some groups, put two monkeys and one pin. In other groups, put one monkey and two pins.

During class, form groups of three. Say: **The Bible says that we should love each other as family. Listen.** Read **1 Peter 3:8** aloud, and have children repeat the verse with you.

Each group is now a family. I'll give each group a set of *plastic monkeys* and *glitter pins*. Divide them among your family members. Each

person who gets a monkey will be an adult. Each person who gets a pin will be a child in your pretend family. You can decide if the adults are moms, dads, or grandparents. You can decide if the kids are boys or girls and how old they are. Once you decide that, come up with a short situation that shows your family acting kindly toward one another. Be ready to act out your situation for the class.

Hand out the monkeys and pins. Circulate among the groups, and be ready to offer help as needed. After three or four minutes, call time, and have groups act out their situations. Then ask:

● **Why is it good for family members to be kind to one another?** (So that everyone gets along; to make families happy.)

● **Should you treat your friends as nicely as you treat your family? Why or why not?** (Yes, because God wants us to; no, I should treat my friends better; no, because families are special.)

● **Are family members always nice to each other? Explain.** (No, sometimes we have fights; no, sometimes one person is selfish; no, sometimes we are in bad moods.)

● **Are friends always nice to each other? Why or why not?** (No, sometimes they get mad at each other; no, sometimes they're jealous.)

● **How do you think God feels when people are unkind to their friends and family?** (It makes God sad; God isn't pleased.)

● **How do you think God feels when people are kind to their friends and family?** (God is happy; God is pleased.)

Say: **Listen to our verse from the Bible. It reminds us of how we should treat our friends.** Read **1 Peter 3:8** aloud, then have children repeat the verse with you. Ask:

● **What can you do to treat your friends as family?** (I can always be kind; I can listen; I can do things they want to do instead of what I want to do.)

Say: **Great ideas! God will be pleased with you when you treat others with such love and kindness. And your friends will be glad, too.** Have children say the Key Verse one more time.

D·E·P·E·N·D·A·B·L·E
F·R·I·E·N·D·S

THE POINT
Good friends can depend on each other.

THE BIBLE BASIS:
1 Samuel 18:1-4. Jonathan and David make a covenant.

Jonathan and all the rest of the Israelites were impressed with David's victory over Goliath. The Bible tells us that Jonathan loved David as much as he loved himself. Jonathan gave some of his favorite possessions to David and made a covenant with him. It was the beginning of a friendship that lasted through incredible trials. Jonathan's father, Saul, hated David, yet Jonathan remained a dependable friend who warned David of Saul's plots against him. David could have sought revenge on Saul by harming his family. But no matter how unfairly Saul treated David, David was always faithful to Jonathan and his children.

David and Jonathan were sincere when they made a covenant to be faithful friends—and they lived by that covenant for years. Our society is so transient that it's hard for children to form friendships that last. True friendships—the kind that last lifetimes—are undeniably precious. Use this lesson to teach your children to be faithful, dependable friends.

Other Scriptures used in this lesson are **Proverbs 17:17a** and **Luke 16:10.**

KEY VERSE
for Lessons 9–13

"…live in harmony with one another; be sympathetic, love as brothers, be compassionate and humble" (1 Peter 3:8).

GETTING THE POINT

Children will

- explore what dependability means,
- play a game in which they depend on their classmates, and
- discover that we count on each other because our lives are interwoven.

Before the lesson, collect the items from the Learning Lab for the activities you plan to use. Refer to the pictures in the margin to see what each item looks like.

THIS LESSON AT A GLANCE

SECTION	MINUTES	WHAT CHILDREN WILL DO	LEARNING LAB SUPPLIES	CLASSROOM SUPPLIES
WELCOME TIME	up to 5	**Welcome!**—Receive a warm welcome from the teacher and make name tags.		"Best Friends Name Tags" (p. 115), scissors, markers, tape or safety pins
ATTENTION GRABBER	up to 10	**Tricks for Two**—Perform stunts that require dependable teamwork and talk about how they depend on their friends.		
BIBLE EXPLORATION & APPLICATION	up to 10	**Friendship Covenant**—Find out about Jonathan and David's covenant from 1 Samuel 18:1-4 and decide what should be included in a friendship covenant.		Bible, newsprint, tape, marker
	up to 15	**Woven Together**—Weave paper together that represents how good friends' lives are interwoven and learn from Proverbs 17:17a that it's important to be loving.	Wikki Stix, felt strips	Bible, construction paper, scissors, markers
	up to 10	**Dependability**—Take apart the crayon car, talk about what makes a car dependable, and compare that to what Luke 16:10 says makes a friend dependable.	Crayon car puzzle	Bible
CLOSING	up to 10	**Trust Your Partner**—Trust partners to keep them from falling and ask God to help them be dependable friends.		

Remember to make photocopies of the "Growing Together" handout (p. 116) to send home with your children. "Growing Together" is a valuable tool for helping first- and second-graders talk with their parents about what they're learning in class.

T·H·E L·E·S·S·O·N

WELCOME TIME

WELCOME!
(up to 5 minutes)

- Greet each child individually with an enthusiastic smile.
- Thank each child for coming to class today.
- As children arrive, ask them about last week's "Growing Together" discussion. Use questions such as "What wise decision did God help you make last week?" and "How did your experiment with the three pans of water help you understand that we need God's wisdom to know what's good?"
- Say: **Today we're going to learn that  good friends can depend on each other.**

THE POINT ★

- Help children make name tags. Photocopy the "Best Friends Name Tags" (p. 115), and follow the instructions.
- Tell children that the attention-getting signal you'll use during this lesson is clapping your hands three times. Ask children to respond by clapping their hands three times as they stop talking and focus their attention on you. Rehearse the signal with the children, telling them to respond quickly so you'll have plenty of time for all the fun activities planned for this lesson.

TTENTION GRABBER

TRICKS FOR TWO
(up to 10 minutes)

Form pairs. Have partners see if they can do the following tricks. Have children switch partners after each trick.

- Trick 1—Have partners face each other and hold each other's hands. Have them turn "inside out" by swinging their arms over their heads and back around to the middle so that they turn completely around. Have them do it slowly once. Then see how many times they can turn inside out without letting go of each other's hands.
- Trick 2—Have partners sit on the floor back to back and link arms. See if they can stand up without letting go of each other.

Teacher Tip

Girls in dresses might be reluctant to try the third trick. That's OK. Just have them switch partners and try one of the first two tricks again.

● Trick 3—Have partners lie down on the floor with their feet touching. See if they can roll across the room with their feet touching.

When everyone has tried the three tricks, get children's attention by clapping your hands three times. Wait for children to respond by clapping three times and focusing their attention on you. Then have them sit on the floor, and ask:

● **What did you like about these tricks?** (They were fun; they were easy; they made me laugh.)

● **What made these tricks hard?** (We couldn't keep our feet together; we kept letting go of our hands; we couldn't figure out how to stand up.)

Say: **In these tricks, both partners had to work together. You depended on your partner to help you.** Ask:

● **What would've happened if you had just stood there, without helping your partner do the tricks?** (My partner would've been mad at me; the trick wouldn't have worked; we wouldn't have had fun.)

● **What do you depend on your friends for in real life?** (I depend on them to have fun with me; to spend time with me; to keep my secrets.)

Say: **We had a lot of fun doing these tricks. Even though we couldn't do all of them perfectly, we had fun because everyone could be depended on to give it a good try.**  **Good friends can depend on each other for a lot of things. Next we're going to find out what two best friends in the Bible did to show that they would be dependable.**

 **THE POINT**

BIBLE EXPLORATION & APPLICATION

FRIENDSHIP COVENANT 📖

(up to 10 minutes)

BIBLE INSIGHT

When Jonathan's soul was "knit" with David's, Jonathan paid a loving tribute to their friendship by giving David his robe and some of his favorite weapons. The gesture was especially touching because the scarceness of weapons at the time had made them particularly valuable.

Tape a sheet of newsprint to the wall so that you can write on it while sitting on the floor. Write "Friendship Covenant" on the top of the newsprint with a marker. Gather the children by the newsprint. Open your Bible to **1 Samuel 18:1-4**, and show the passage to the children.

Say: **The two people in our Bible story had reason to dislike each other, but they were best friends. David could've hated Jonathan, because Jonathan's father, King Saul, wanted to kill David. Jonathan could've hated David because Jonathan was next in line to be king, but God said that David was to be the next king instead.**

The Bible says that Jonathan loved David as much as he loved himself. Jonathan even gave David presents to show how much he liked him. He gave David his coat, his battle armor, his sword, his bow to shoot arrows with, and his belt. They were wonderful presents, and David was very glad Jonathan gave them to him.

But David was even happier because he and Jonathan made a promise to be friends. The Bible calls their promise a covenant, or an agreement. In a covenant, two people make a promise to each other. Today we call covenants contracts. Let's pretend that we were there when Jonathan and David made their covenant. Ask:

● **What do you think they promised each other?** (To protect each other; to be kind to each other; to keep their promises; to keep each other's secrets.)

Write down each child's idea on the newsprint.

● **What promises should we make to our friends today?** (To have fun together; to be nice to each other; to play together.)

Write down each child's idea on the newsprint.

Say: **Promises are special, so David and Jonathan were careful to always keep the covenant of friendship they made to each other. They knew they could depend on each other. From that time on, whenever David needed help escaping from Saul, Jonathan helped him. And David kept the covenant even after Jonathan died. David was kind to Jonathan's children because he had loved Jonathan so much. Jonathan and David were good friends, and they knew that ✦ good friends can depend on each other.**

THE POINT

WOVEN TOGETHER 📖

(up to 15 minutes)

For each child, fold an 8½×11 sheet of construction paper in half. Cut about six slits in the paper from the fold to near the edge, leaving a margin of an inch at the end of the slits. See the drawing in the margin. Cut short strips from additional sheets of construction paper that will be woven through the slits of the 8½×11 sheets of paper.

In class, set out the sheets of paper with the slits cut in them, paper strips, *Wikki Stix, felt strips,* and markers.

Give each child several paper strips and a marker. Have children write their friends' names on the strips. Then, beside each name, have them write one good friendship quality that friend has. For example, on one slip someone might write, "Chris—fun to play with." Encourage children to include family members as friends.

Have each child choose a sheet of paper with slits cut in it and write his or her name on top. Then have children weave their paper strips into the slits. Show them how to alternate the strips over and under the slits.

Also have them weave in *felt strips* and pieces of *Wikki Stix.* Explain that the *felt strips* are to remind them of how soft and comforting a good friendship can be. The *Wikki Stix* are to remind them how loyal friends are—friends stick together.

While the children are weaving, ask:

★ **THE POINT**

● **How do you know that you can depend on your friends?** (Because they're nice to me; because they're my friends; because that's what friends do.)

● **How does it make you feel to know that you can count on your friends?** (It makes me feel that I can trust them; it makes me feel good.)

Say: **Look at your paper weavings. Pretend the big piece of paper is you. The little pieces of paper are your friends. We've woven them together to show that we can count on each other.** Ask:

● **What would happen if one of these slips of paper got ripped?** (There would be a big hole in the picture; it could ruin the picture.)

Say: **Sometimes we mess up and aren't dependable, or our friends mess up and aren't very dependable. That causes holes in our friendships just as it would cause holes in our weavings. Weavings that have holes aren't as strong as weavings without holes.** Ask:

● **What would you do if there were a hole in your weaving?** (I'd tape it together; I'd fix it; I'd make a new weaving.)

● **What can you do if there's a hole in your friendship that happened because someone wasn't dependable?** (I could say I was sorry; I could forgive my friend; I could fix the friendship.)

Say: **It's important to fix the holes in our friendships. We can forgive each other when we're not dependable. Then we can try even harder to be friends who can be counted on.**

These paper weavings show how we depend on our friends. Your papers are woven with your friends' slips. That means your friends are depending on you, too. Listen to what the Bible says about being a good friend. Read **Proverbs 17:17a.**

Say: **Friends love each other all the time. Part of being friends is loving each other and counting on each other.** ★ **Good friends can depend on each other.**

The children can take their weavings home with them.

DEPENDABILITY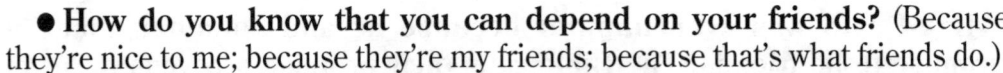

(up to 10 minutes)

Take the *crayon car puzzle* apart, and give the pieces to the children. If you have more than eight children, have some of them pair up and share a puzzle piece. Ask:

● **What's the most important part of a car?** (The wheels; the engine; the gas tank.)

● **What would happen if a car didn't have that piece?** (The car couldn't go anywhere; it wouldn't run; there would be no place to put the gas.)

When we ride in a car, we depend on it to get us where we're going. If an important part of the car is missing, the car might not be dependable. Ask:

● **What happens if a car isn't dependable?** (We can't get where we're going; it might get stuck somewhere.)

● **What's it like to have a friend who isn't dependable?** (It's no fun; I never know if I can count on her; I don't want to trust him.)

● **How would you feel if your friends kept their promises to you some of the time but broke their promises the rest of the time?** (I'd be mad; I wouldn't trust them.)

● **What would your friends think if you kept their secrets some of the time but told them to others the rest of the time?** (They wouldn't want to be friends with me anymore; they wouldn't tell me any more secrets.)

● **What can we do to be dependable friends?** (We can always keep our promises; we can be kind to our friends all the time; we can share.)

Have the children put the *crayon car puzzle* together.

Say: **If a car doesn't start every once in a while, we're afraid to trust it because we never know when it will work and when it won't. It's the same way with friends. We need to be trustworthy all the time. Listen to what the Bible says.** Read **Luke 16:10** aloud. **When we're trustworthy all the time, our friends can count on us. And ✦ good friends can depend on each other.**

THE POINT

We believe that Christian education extends beyond the classroom into the home. Photocopy the "Growing Together" handout (p. 116) for this week, and send it home with your children. Encourage children and parents to use the handout to plan meaningful activities on this week's topic. Follow up the "Growing Together" activities next week by asking children what their families did together.

CLOSING

TRUST YOUR PARTNER
(up to 10 minutes)

Ask:

● **What did you learn today?** (I learned that I should be trustworthy; I learned that I should be dependable; I learned that good friends can depend on each other.)

Form pairs. Have partners squat facing each other, join hands, and lean back. Encourage children to hold tightly because if either partner lets go, both of them will fall over. After all the children have tried it, have them shake hands and say, "Thanks for being a dependable friend."

Gather the children together and ask:

● **How did it feel to depend on your friend?** (It was scary; it was fun.)

● **Did you worry that you might fall? Explain.** (A little, but I could count on my friend; no, I knew he wouldn't let me down.)

● **How would you have felt if your partner had let you fall?** (I would've been mad; I would've been upset, but I would have forgiven her.)

Say: **You depended on your partner to help you stay upright in this activity. We depend on our friends every day in real life. And we hope that our friends are dependable so we don't end up getting hurt. Let's ask God to help us be dependable so that our friends can count on us.**

Pray: **God, we know that** ★ **good friends can depend on each other. We ask you to help us always be dependable friends. Thank you for being our dependable friend. In Jesus' name, amen.**

BEST FRIENDS NAME TAGS

Photocopy this page. Cut apart the name tags, and give one to each child. Have each child color one face to look like himself or herself and the other face to look like his or her best friend. Help the children write their names and their friends' names on the blanks.

Me: _____

My friend: _____

Me: _____

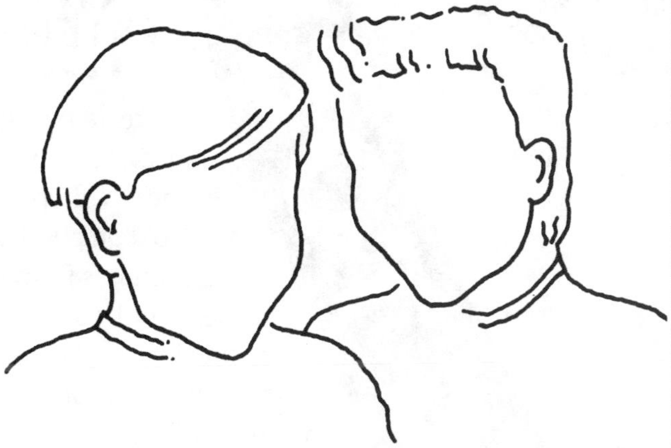

My friend: _____

Me: _____

My friend: _____

Me: _____

My friend: _____

FRIENDSHIP 9:

Good friends can depend on each other.

KEY VERSE

"...live in harmony with one another; be sympathetic, love as brothers, be compassionate and humble" (1 Peter 3:8).

GROWING TOGETHER

I·N T·O·U·C·H

Today your child learned that it's important to be dependable. The children found out that Jonathan and David made an agreement to be good friends and they stuck by their commitment. Use these activities at home to teach your child to be a dependable friend.

FAR-AWAY FRIENDS

Create new greeting cards to send to friends. Cut pictures from old greeting cards, or clip photos from magazines. Fold construction paper in half, and glue a picture to the front. Start a new family tradition: As soon as Sunday dinner is finished, write a greeting to a friend or family member, and send it to teach your child to be faithful to faraway friends as well as nearby friends.

DEPENDABLE CANDIES

Make these easy turtle candies. Line a baking sheet with buttered foil. For each candy, place 3 pecan halves in a Y-shape on the foil with the edges almost touching. Put a caramel candy in the middle of the Y-shape. Bake in a 300° oven about 10 minutes or until the caramels melt. While caramels are melting, melt a 6-ounce package of chocolate chips and a teaspoon of shortening in a saucepan on low heat. Take the candies out of the oven, and spread a spoonful of chocolate over each caramel. Refrigerate until the chocolate is firm. Talk about how the candies are held together by the melted caramel and how good friendships are held together by dependability.

YESTERDAY'S FAITHFUL

Celebrate All Saints' Day on November 1. God used the Christians of yesterday to pass on the faith to Christians of today. Choose a famous Christian such as Francis of Assisi, William Carey, Billy Graham, Martin Luther, or Corrie ten Boom. Get information about that person from your church library or from your public library. Find out how Christianity has been made richer by his or her contribution, and thank God for that person's life of faith. Ask for God's help in developing your family's faith so that the next generation of Christians can depend on you. Explain to your child how important it is for each generation to carry the message of God to the next generation.

GOOD NEIGHBORS

Being a dependable neighbor is one way to be a dependable friend. Be secret good neighbors. One day you might  secretly clean your neighbors' car windows with window cleaner and paper towels or old newspapers. First make sure they don't have a car alarm! Another time you might rake your neighbors' leaves. Or you could shovel snow from their sidewalk. Be sure not to tell—the fun is in keeping the secret.

J·O·Y·F·U·L
F·R·I·E·N·D·S

THE POINT
Good friends are happy for each other.

THE BIBLE BASIS:
1 Samuel 19:1-7. Jonathan defends David's victories to Saul.

David caused a lot of upset in Jonathan's household. Jonathan's father, King Saul, was so upset by David's public support that he vowed to kill David. Saul ordered his servants and his son to kill David at the first opportunity. But Jonathan defied the royal order and praised David's actions. Jonathan bravely stood up to his father and reminded him that David acted in service to God and the king. David had no ill will against the king.

Jonathan demonstrated that part of the promise of friendship is to believe wholeheartedly in our friends—to be proud of their accomplishments and do all we can to support them. Jonathan could have been jealous of David's accomplishments. David was praised in the streets for slaying tens of thousands of Israel's enemies. David was a skilled musician. He was handsome and loved.

But Jonathan's friendship was pure. Jonathan was truly happy for his friend and did his best to protect David from harm. That's the kind of friend God wants your students to be. This lesson will teach children to support their friends and to be genuinely happy for them.

Other Scriptures used in this lesson are **Galatians 5:26** and **Romans 12:15a.**

KEY VERSE
for Lessons 9–13

"…live in harmony with one another; be sympathetic, love as brothers, be compassionate and humble" (1 Peter 3:8).

GETTING THE POINT

Children will

- practice being happy for each other,
- find out that jealousy damages friendships, and
- discover that being happy for friends means to support and encourage them.

Before the lesson, collect the items from the Learning Lab for the activities you plan to use. Refer to the pictures in the margin to see what each item looks like.

THIS LESSON AT A GLANCE

SECTION	MINUTES	WHAT CHILDREN WILL DO	LEARNING LAB SUPPLIES	CLASSROOM SUPPLIES
WELCOME TIME	up to 5	**Welcome!**—Receive a warm welcome from the teacher and make name tags.		"Best Friends Name Tags" (p. 115), scissors, markers, tape or safety pins
ATTENTION GRABBER	up to 10	**Puppet Cheers**—Cheer on a puppet for a great accomplishment and learn that being happy for a friend feels good.	Hand puppet, plastic rings	
BIBLE EXPLORATION & APPLICATION	up to 10	**Jonathan Saves David**—Listen to the story from 1 Samuel 19:1-7 of how Jonathan saved David's life by praising him to Saul.		Bible
	up to 10	**Inner Support**—Find out that important roles often aren't seen and learn from Galatians 5:26 that they can be happy for friends instead of jealous.	Crayon car puzzle	Bible
	up to 15	**Cheer Them On**—Play a game similar to Musical Chairs to practice being happy for friends and learn from Romans 12:15a that they can rejoice with those who are happy.	Cassette: "Good Friends Music"	Bible, cassette player, paper, marker
CLOSING	up to 10	**Everything's Better With a Friend**—Sing a song about friendship, thank God for friends, and ask for help in being happy for their friends.	Cassette: "Everything's Better With a Friend," "Lyrics Poster"	Cassette player

Remember to make photocopies of the "Growing Together" handout (p. 124) to send home with your children. "Growing Together" is a valuable tool for helping first- and second-graders talk with their parents about what they're learning in class.

ELCOME TIME

WELCOME!

(up to 5 minutes)

- Greet each child individually with an enthusiastic smile.
- Thank each child for coming to class today.
- As children arrive, ask them about last week's "Growing Together" discussion. Use questions such as "In what ways were you a dependable friend to someone last week?" and "How did you secretly help your neighbor last week?"
- Say: **Today we're going to learn that** ✦ **good friends are happy for each other.**
- Hand out the name tags children made during Lesson 9, and help them attach the name tags to their clothing. If some of the name tags were damaged, or if children weren't in class that week, have them make new name tags using the photocopiable handout on page 115.
- Tell children that the attention-getting signal you'll use during this lesson is clapping your hands three times. Ask children to respond by clapping their hands three times as they stop talking and focus their attention on you. Rehearse the signal with the children, telling them to respond quickly so you'll have plenty of time for all the fun activities planned for this lesson.

THE POINT ✦

TTENTION GRABBER

PUPPET CHEERS

(up to 10 minutes)

LEARNING LAB

Have children form a line. Have the first person walk about 10 feet away from the line and turn around to face the second person in line. Give the first person the *hand puppet*. Give the *plastic rings* to the second person in line.

Have the person with the rings toss them one at a time to the person with the puppet. Have the person with the puppet try to catch the rings in the puppet's mouth. Every time the puppet catches a ring, have the class cheer for the puppet by saying things such as "Way to go, puppet!"

When all five rings have been tossed, have the ring thrower become the puppet holder. Have the first puppet holder give the rings to the next person and go to the end of the line. Play until every child has had a turn to throw the rings and hold the puppet. Put away the *hand puppet* and *plastic rings*.

Get the children's attention by clapping three times. Wait for the children to clap three times and focus their attention on you. Have children sit on the floor. Ask:

● **What was it like to cheer for the puppet?** (It was fun; I felt silly because the puppet isn't real.)

● **Why do you cheer for friends in real life?** (Because it's fun; it makes me feel good because it makes them feel good.)

● **Was the puppet the one who deserved our praise, or was it the person whose hand was inside the puppet? Explain.** (The puppet, because it caught the rings; the person, because she made the puppet catch the rings.)

 **THE POINT**

Say: **It's fun to cheer for our friends because** ✦ **good friends are happy for each other. The people holding the puppet were really the ones who deserved the praise, but they could listen to the praise that the puppet got and feel good. Today our story is about a person who helped his friend and was happy for his friend, even though he didn't get very much credit. Let's find out what happened.**

BIBLE EXPLORATION & APPLICATION

JONATHAN SAVES DAVID 📖

(up to 10 minutes)

Open your Bible to **1 Samuel 19:1-7,** and show the passage to the children. Say: **This story is about three people. I'm going to teach you a sound to make when each person is mentioned. When I talk about Saul, pound your fists on the floor three times because he was powerful, noisy, and mean. Let's try that. Saul.** Pause for children to pound their fists on the floor.

Good! When I mention David, clap your hands together really fast. David was running away from Saul. His heart was probably beating really quickly because he was scared and he was running. Let's try that. David. Pause for children to clap their hands quickly.

Great! When I mention Jonathan, rub your hands together softly because he was the peacemaker who smoothed things out between Saul and David. Let's try that. Jonathan. Pause for children to rub their hands together softly.

Super! Here's the story: Saul (pause) **told his son Jonathan** (pause) **and all the servants to kill David** (pause) **the first chance they got. But**

Jonathan (pause) **liked David** (pause) **very much, so Jonathan** (pause) **warned David** (pause). **He said, "My father, Saul,** (pause) **is looking for a chance to kill you. Go and hide in a secret place. I'll talk to my father and find out what he plans to do. Then I'll tell you about his plans.**

When Jonathan (pause) **talked to Saul** (pause), **Jonathan** (pause) **told him about all the wonderful things David** (pause) **had done. Jonathan** (pause) **said, "You shouldn't hurt David** (pause) **because he hasn't done anything wrong to you. In fact, he's even helped you. David** (pause) **risked his life to kill Goliath so that you would win a great victory for the entire country. You saw it, and you were glad he killed Goliath. Why would you hurt such a good person? David** (pause) **is innocent. There's no reason to hurt him.**

Saul (pause) **listened to Jonathan** (pause) **and agreed with him. Saul** (pause) **made this promise: "As surely as God lives, David** (pause) **won't be killed."**

Now let's rub our hands softly for each person because things were smoothed out.

Jonathan (pause) **called out to David** (pause) **and told him everything that had happened. Jonathan** (pause) **brought Saul** (pause) **and David** (pause) **together, and there was peace.** Ask:

● **How do you think Jonathan felt when Saul decided not to kill David?** (He was happy for David; he was glad his plan had worked.)

Say: **Jonathan was a prince—the son of the king. But David got more attention than Jonathan did. Jonathan could've been jealous, but he was happy for all the good things David had done. Jonathan was happy that David had killed Goliath. He was happy that David had done so many things for his country.** Ask:

● **Have you ever been jealous of a friend who did all kinds of good things? What does that feel like?** (It feels bad; it makes me sad; it makes me feel that my friend is better than me; it makes me feel that I can't do anything right.)

Say: **It's easy to be jealous of our friends. God understands that we want to feel special too. But God also wants us to love and be happy for our friends, even when they get more attention than we do. God wants ✦ good friends to be happy for each other.**

INNER SUPPORT 📖

(up to 10 minutes)

Show children the *crayon car puzzle*. Say: **An important part of this puzzle can't be seen. It's the support that's inside the puzzle that holds it all together.**

Take the puzzle apart, and show the children the support. Put the puzzle back together, but leave out the support piece. Have the children try to "drive" the car along the floor or table top without the support. Then put the puzzle

THE POINT ⭐

LEARNING LAB

together with the support, and have the children drive it along the floor or table top.

Say: **Even though we can't see the support when the crayon car is put together, we know that the support is important. It was the same with Jonathan and David. Jonathan was David's support. Jonathan helped David and kept him safe. He persuaded Saul not to kill David.**

But David was the one who got all the people's praise. All the people of Israel loved David. Jonathan was happy for David instead of being jealous. God wants ★ good friends to be happy for each other, even when one friend gets more attention than the other. Listen to what the Bible says about jealousy. Read **Galatians 5:26** aloud.

 **THE POINT**

Say: **Instead of being jealous of our friends, we can be happy for them and support them. I know all of you can be good, supporting friends.** Ask:

● **What can you do to support your friends?** (I can stick up for them; I can be happy when they win awards; I can be happy when they beat me at Checkers; I can say good things about them to others.)

● **When do your friends need your support?** (When people are mean to them; when they're sad; when they need help; all the time.)

● **What can you do to be happy for your friends?** (I can say, "Good job!" when they beat me; I can congratulate them when they win awards; I can stop being jealous.)

 **THE POINT**

Say: ★ **Good friends are happy for each other. That means we do whatever we can to praise our friends. Our support, praise, and happiness for our friends makes them strong inside just as the support inside this car makes it strong.**

Return the *crayon car puzzle* to the Learning Lab.

CHEER THEM ON 📖
(up to 15 minutes)

Draw a happy face on a sheet of paper. Shuffle it with enough other sheets of paper for every child to have one. Hand out the sheets of paper. Have children stand in a circle and put the sheets of paper on the floor in front of them. Cue the *cassette tape* to "Good Friends Music."

Say: **Listen to what the Bible says about being happy for our friends.** Read **Romans 12:15a** aloud. **Let's be happy for our friends right now.**

Have children walk around the circle while the music plays. The music has intermittent pauses. Each time the music pauses, stop the tape, and have the class cheer for whoever is standing next to the paper with the happy face. Then have that child sit in the middle of the circle and take one blank piece of paper out of the circle. Start the tape again. Play until all the children have been cheered.

Stop the tape and ask:

Teacher Tip

There are 18 pauses in this cassette tape segment. If you have more than 18 students, rewind the tape so there's music for the children who haven't had a turn yet.

● **Did you like being cheered? Explain.** (Yes, it felt good; no, I was embarrassed; yes, because I felt that my friends cared for me.)

● **What else can you do to show your friends that you're happy for them?** (I can throw a birthday party for my friend; I can smile at them; I can tell my teacher about how my friend helps me.)

Have children pass around the paper with the happy face. As they hold the paper, have them tell something they'll do to cheer a friend this week.

Say: **God is pleased with you for cheering for each other and for all of your good ideas about being happy for your friends. You've shown that ✦ good friends are happy for each other.**

THE POINT ✦

W̲e believe that Christian education extends beyond the classroom into the home.  Photocopy the "Growing Together" handout (p. 124) for this week, and send it home with your children. Encourage children and parents to use the handout to plan meaningful activities on this week's topic. Follow up the "Growing Together" activities next week by asking children what their families did together.

CLOSING

EVERYTHING'S BETTER WITH A FRIEND
(up to 10 minutes)

Ask:

● **What did you learn today?** (I learned to not be jealous of my friends; I learned to be happy when my friends do something good; I learned to help my friends however I can.)

Cue the *cassette tape* to "Everything's Better With a Friend." Choose a volunteer to hold the "Lyrics Poster." Choose another volunteer to point to the words as you sing them. Sing the song with the class.

Then say: ✦ **Good friends are happy for each other. They stand up for each other, and they're always proud of their friends. Let's thank God for our friends.**

Pray: **God, friendship is a wonderful gift that you've given us. Thank you for giving us good friends, and help us to be happy for them and proud of them. In Jesus' name, amen.**

THE POINT ✦

FRIENDSHIP 10:

Good friends are happy for each other.

KEY VERSE

"...live in harmony with one another; be sympathetic, love as brothers, be compassionate and humble" (1 Peter 3:8).

GROWING TOGETHER

I·N T·O·U·C·H

Today your child learned to be happy for friends. Being happy for friends means appreciating them for their strengths, supporting them in front of others, and being joyous when they accomplish good things. Use these activities to help your child develop good friendships.

MAKE FRIENDS

The world is full of new friends! Teach your child how to find them. Encourage your child to make new friends by inviting others over to play or seeking them out on the playground. Have your child practice being happy for a new friend by listing all the qualities that make him or her special. Practice what you preach by making friends with a new family at church. Invite them over for a soup or salad supper. Thank God for providing new friends.

HAPPY MEMORIES

Take pictures of your child playing with his or her friends when they come over to your house. When birthday parties come around, slip a picture of the children in with the birthday card.

HAPPY TREATS

Have your child make and share this healthy treat with a friend. It will make both of them happy. Cut an apple into bite-sized chunks. Place it in a dish, sprinkle it with cinnamon, cover it, and microwave it on high for two minutes. Sprinkle it with raisins and nuts, and top it with vanilla ice cream.

BUBBLY REWARDS

Congratulate your child for an accomplishment such as losing a tooth or learning to spell a tough word. Give each family member a bottle of bubble solution and a bubble wand. Give the signal, and have your family bombard your child with cascades of soap bubbles while singing, "For (child's name)'s a jolly, good winner."

W·O·R·K
I·T O·U·T

THE POINT
Good friends work out problems with each other.

THE BIBLE BASIS:

1 Samuel 20:1-23. Saul nearly comes between David and Jonathan.

Jonathan and David had a problem that few best friends face—Jonathan's dad was trying to murder David. Several times David escaped Saul's plot or Jonathan persuaded his father to abandon his plan. But Saul kept returning to the idea that David was his enemy. In this episode, David ran to Jonathan for help. When Jonathan and David put their heads together, they came up with a plan to help David escape from Saul once again. The friends were successful: When Jonathan found that Saul was ready to attack David, he got word to David, who was hiding in the fields.

Friends are great to have around when we need help to solve a tough problem. They care about us, so they're motivated to do whatever they can to help. Ecclesiastes 4:9-10 says, "Two people are better than one, because they get more done by working together. If one falls down, the other can help him up. But it is bad for the person who is alone and falls, because no one is there to help." Children need to learn to be ready to assist when their friends need help. Use this lesson to teach children to work together to solve problems and accomplish difficult tasks.

Other Scriptures used in this lesson are **Ecclesiastes 4:9-10; Galatians 6:2;** and **1 Peter 3:8.**

KEY VERSE
for Lessons 9–13

"…live in harmony with one another; be sympathetic, love as brothers, be compassionate and humble" (1 Peter 3:8).

GETTING THE POINT

Children will

- find out that problems are easier to solve with help from a friend,
- discover what to do when friends have problems with each other, and
- learn that problems aren't always as difficult and complicated as they seem.

Before the lesson, collect the items from the Learning Lab for the activities you plan to use. Refer to the pictures in the margin to see what each item looks like.

THIS LESSON AT A GLANCE

SECTION	MINUTES	WHAT CHILDREN WILL DO	LEARNING LAB SUPPLIES	CLASSROOM SUPPLIES
WELCOME TIME	up to 5	**Welcome!**—Receive a warm welcome from the teacher and make name tags.		"Best Friends Name Tags" (p. 115), scissors, markers, tape or safety pins
ATTENTION GRABBER	up to 10	**A Tough Problem**—Figure out how to make a wheel bounce without touching it and talk about the problems they face.	Learning Lab items	
BIBLE EXPLORATION & APPLICATION	up to 10	**A Friendly Plan**—Listen to a story from 1 Samuel 20:1-17 and find out about the plan David and Jonathan made to work out a problem.		Bible
	up to 12	**Cooperation**—Cooperate in a game, talk about the things that at least two people are needed to do, and learn from Ecclesiastes 4:9-10 that two people are better than one.	Flower foam	Bible, tape, newsprint, marker
	up to 13	**Friends?**—Listen to a story about a misunderstanding, find out that things aren't always what they seem, and learn from 1 Peter 3:8 that it's important to live in harmony.	Cassette: "Friends?," dart blower	Bible, cassette player
CLOSING	up to 10	**Togetherness**—Help a friend with a task, hear Galatians 6:2, and ask God to help them solve problems with their friends.		Bible, paper, markers

Remember to make photocopies of the "Growing Together" handout (p. 133) to send home with your children. "Growing Together" is a valuable tool for helping first- and second-graders talk with their parents about what they're learning in class.

ELCOME TIME

WELCOME!
(up to 5 minutes)

- Greet each child individually with an enthusiastic smile.
- Thank each child for coming to class today.
- As children arrive, ask them about last week's "Growing Together" discussion. Use questions such as "What was it like to make a new friend last week?" and "How did the bubbly rewards you received from your family make you feel?"
- Say: **Today we're going to learn that** ✭ **good friends work out problems with each other.**

THE POINT ✭

- Hand out the name tags children made during Lesson 9, and help them attach the name tags to their clothing. If some of the name tags were damaged, or if children weren't in class that week, have them make new name tags using the photocopiable handout on page 115.
- Tell children that the attention-getting signal you'll use during this lesson is clapping your hands three times. Ask children to respond by clapping their hands three times as they stop talking and focus their attention on you. Rehearse the signal with the children, telling them to respond quickly so you'll have plenty of time for all the fun activities planned for this lesson.

TTENTION GRABBER

A TOUGH PROBLEM
(up to 10 minutes)

Have children sit in a circle on the floor. Put the Learning Lab in the center of the circle. Take out the *super bouncing wheel,* and say: **I've got a puzzle for you to figure out. It's possible to bounce this wheel without touching it with your hands. Let's see if you can figure out how to do it. You can use any of the Learning Lab supplies.**

Place the wheel flat on the floor. Give children a few minutes to figure it out. If they can't, show them that the wheel bounces when it's hit with the *dart*

LEARNING LAB

blower. Let all the children try it. Then put the Learning Lab away. Ask:

● **Was this a hard puzzle to solve? Why or why not?** (Yes, I didn't think it was possible; no, the *dart blower* was the only thing that worked.)

● **What kinds of hard puzzles or problems do you have to solve in real life?** (I have a 100-piece puzzle that's really hard to do; I have trouble with subtraction; I have trouble remembering which letters are silent.)

● **What do you do when you have to solve a tough problem?** (I work really hard; I try to find the answer; I ask someone to help me.)

Say: **All of us come across tough problems that need to be solved. One of the best things about having friends is that they can help us.**  **Good friends work out problems together. Today we're going to find out about two friends who faced a huge problem. We'll find out what they did to solve it.**

 **THE POINT**

BIBLE EXPLORATION & APPLICATION

A FRIENDLY PLAN 📖
(up to 10 minutes)

Form pairs. In each pair, have partners decide who will be David and who will be Jonathan.

Open your Bible to **1 Samuel 20:1-23,** and show children the passage. Keep your Bible open in front of you. Say: **In this story, Jonathan and David have a problem to solve. Every time David says something to explain the problem or to help solve the problem, all the Davids should stick out one hand. When Jonathan says something to explain or solve the problem, all the Jonathans should stick out a hand and put it on top of their partners' hands. Keep stacking your hands on top of each other's hands. When you run out of hands, move one hand from the bottom up to the top. Here's the story:**

Once again Saul decided to kill David, so David ran to Jonathan for help. David was very upset. He asked: "Jonathan, what have I done? What is my crime? What have I done to your father that would make him want to kill me?" Pause.

Jonathan said, "Don't worry. You won't die. See, my father doesn't do anything without telling me. If he were going to kill you, I'd know about it." Pause.

But David said: "Don't you see? Your father knows that we're friends. He won't tell you if he wants to kill me, because he knows that you'll tell me and I'll escape. I'm sure he's going to kill me." Pause.

Jonathan asked, "What can I do to help you escape?" Pause.

David said, "Tomorrow is the New Moon festival. I'm supposed to eat with the king. But I'm going to hide in the fields instead. If your father notices that I'm gone, tell him I've gone to Bethlehem to be with my family. If your father says 'fine,' then it's OK, and I'm safe. But if he gets angry, you'll know that he means to kill me." Pause.

Jonathan said, "If I find out that he plans to hurt you, I'll warn you." Pause.

But David said, "Who will let me know if your father answers unkindly?" Pause.

Jonathan said: "I promise before the Lord God of Israel that I'll find out if my father is going to kill you. I promise that I'll tell you if he feels good toward you. And if he means to hurt you, I'll send you away safely. This is how you'll know.

"When I find out what my father is going to do, I'll shoot three arrows into the field where you're hiding. Then I'll send someone to go bring them back. If I say to him, 'The arrows are nearby; bring them here,' you'll know that you're safe. But if I say, 'The arrows are far away; keep going,' then you'll know that you must go away." Pause.

Then Jonathan and David promised again to be good friends forever. They had worked together to find a way to save David from Saul again. Ask:

● **How do you think David felt when Jonathan helped him with his problem?** (Good; happy that Jonathan cared about him; glad, because he wouldn't be killed.)

● **What problems have you worked out with a friend?** (I helped my friend clean her room once; my friend helped me when some big kids were being mean to me.)

● **What happens to your friendship when you solve a problem together?** (It grows stronger; we're better friends than ever.)

Say: **Jonathan helped David because they were good friends.** ✦ **Good friends work out problems with each other. We can help our friends too. Let's find out how to work together to solve problems.**

THE POINT ★

COOPERATION 📖

(up to 12 minutes)

Tape two sheets of newsprint to the wall.

Choose one volunteer to be "It." Have the rest of the children form a circle and link arms. Tape a piece of *flower foam* to one child's back. Have It stand on the outside of the circle opposite the child with the foam. Say: **When I say "go," It will try to tag the *flower foam*. You can move the circle to the right or to the left to keep It away from the foam, but you all must stay in the circle and keep your arms linked together. Ready? Go!**

Play the game until It tags the foam. Then choose another It and another volunteer to wear the foam and play again. After several rounds of the game, put

LEARNING LAB

★ THE POINT

away the *flower foam,* and have the children sit down. Ask:

● **How did you work together to keep It from tagging the foam?** (I pulled when we needed to go the other direction; I called out to the other side that we needed to hurry; I kept my friend from falling.)

● **Was working together important in this game? Why or why not?** (Yes, if we didn't work together, It would have tagged the foam; yes, my teammates helped me know where It was.)

Say: **Cooperation can be fun. And there are some things that we can't do unless we work with someone else.** Ask:

● **What kinds of things does it take at least two people to do?** (Play Tag; have a pillow fight; run a race; go for piggyback rides.)

Write children's answers on the newsprint.

Say: **You all had to work together to keep It from tagging the *flower foam.* If you hadn't worked together, It would have won the game quickly every time. Cooperation makes things easier and more fun. That's especially true when we have problems to work out. God says that two people are better than one. Listen to what the Bible says, and be ready to tell me what two people can do together.** Read **Ecclesiastes 4:9-10.** Ask:

● **What can two people do together?** (Get more done; help each other up.)

Say: ★ **Good friends work out problems with each other because they know that problems are solved more quickly when they have a friend to help.**

FRIENDS? 📖

(up to 13 minutes)

Cue the *cassette tape* to the "Friends?" segment. Have children sit on the floor. Say: **Listen to this story about two friends.**

Play part 1 of "Friends?" When part 1 ends, turn off the tape, and ask:

● **Why do you think Jerry and Stacy wouldn't play with Spencer?** (Maybe they didn't like him anymore; maybe they got in trouble, and their moms wouldn't let them play.)

● **What do you think will happen to their friendship?** (I bet they stop being friends; I think they'll forgive each other.)

Say: **It sure seems like there's trouble between these friends. But things aren't always what they seem. Before we listen to the end of the story, I want to show you something else that isn't what it seems.**

Have children take turns holding the *dart blower* in front of one eye and holding the other hand behind the *dart blower* with the palm facing in. If the children keep both eyes open, they'll see a hole in the middle of their hands. Pass around the *dart blower,* and let all the children try it. Warn them not to hold the *dart blower* too close to their eyes. Then put away the *dart blower,* and ask:

● **What did you see when you looked through the *dart blower*?** (I saw a hole in my hand.)

Say: **We all know that we don't have holes in our hands—even though we *saw* the holes. Things aren't always the way we think they are. That's why we need to work out our problems with our friends and get to the bottom of things. Let's find out what really happened in the story.**

Play part 2 of "Friends?" After the segment, turn off the tape and ask:

● **How do you think Spencer felt when he found out the truth?** (He was happy; he was surprised; I think he was sorry he had been mad at his friends.)

Say: **Listen to what the Bible says about how we should treat our friends.** Read **1 Peter 3:8,** then ask:

● **Why is it important to get all of the facts before you get mad at someone?** (So you don't get mad when your friends are doing something nice for you; so you don't make a mistake.)

Say: **Sometimes it's easy to jump to conclusions and get mad. Spencer thought that Stacy and Jerry didn't want to be friends anymore, but he found out that they were really good friends who cared about him a lot. Spencer, Stacy, and Jerry worked out their misunderstanding and remained good friends.** ✦ **Good friends work out problems with each other—they work things out instead of jumping to conclusions.**

THE POINT

We believe that Christian education extends beyond the classroom into the home. Photocopy the "Growing Together" handout (p. 133) for this week, and send it home with your children. Encourage children and parents to use the handout to plan meaningful activities on this week's topic. Follow up the "Growing Together" activities next week by asking children what their families did together.

CLOSING

TOGETHERNESS 📖

(up to 10 minutes)

Ask:

● **What did you learn today?** (I learned that things are better with two people; I learned to help my friends solve problems; I learned to cooperate.)

Form pairs. Give each pair two sheets of paper and one marker. Say: **Choose** one partner to go first. That partner gets the marker. Hold the marker in the hand you don't usually write with. The other partner will guide your hand to write the word "friend" on the paper.

Write the word "friend" on a piece of paper so children can see how it's spelled. When the children are finished writing, have them switch roles and write the same word on the other piece of paper.

**THE POINT**

Then say: **You all did a great job of helping each other. You really know how to cooperate!** ✦ **Good friends work out problems with each other, and they do it by cooperating. Tell your partner one thing you'll do this week to help a friend with a problem.**

Give children a moment to share. Then have volunteers tell the class what they'll do.

Say: **Great ideas! Listen to what the Bible says about helping each other.** Read **Galatians 6:2** aloud. **Let's ask God to help us help our friends.**

Pray: **God, thank you for giving us friends. We know the Bible says that two people are better than one. We want to help our friends this week by working together. Please help us work out problems with our friends. In Jesus' name, amen.**

FRIENDSHIP 11:

Good friends work out problems with each other.

KEY VERSE

"...live in harmony with one another; be sympathetic, love as brothers, be compassionate and humble" (1 Peter 3:8).

GROWING TOGETHER

Today your child learned that problems are more easily solved when people work together. The children learned to cooperate and to work things out when they have misunderstandings with each other. Use these activities to teach your child to work with his or her friends.

TUMMY HUGS

Enjoy this tummy-warming, maple-cinnamon drink while you tackle a tough problem with your child. Put 2 mugfuls of milk in a saucepan over medium heat. Add 3 or 4 generous tablespoons of pancake syrup, a little vanilla flavoring, and a sprinkle of cinnamon and nutmeg. Heat until steaming. Mmm!

TACKLE A PROBLEM

Help your child become a caring problem-solver. Watch the news together, then choose a problem that faces society, such as homelessness, the national deficit, hunger, or crime. Work with your child to think of ideas to ease or solve the problem. What should governments do to solve the problem? What should churches do to solve the problem? What should your family do to solve the problem? Choose at least one action for your family to take.

PROBLEM SOLVER

Even the best of friends sometimes have problems with each other. Encourage your child to use this problem-solving technique. When your child has an argument with a friend, have him or her give the other child a chance to say what's wrong without interrupting. Then have your child repeat what was said in his or her own words. Then give your child the same chance to explain what's wrong. Have the friend repeat what he or she heard. Then have both children decide what would be fair for the other child, and help them reach a compromise. Encourage them to say, "I'm sorry."

READY TO HELP

Have each family member write down a list of chores and problems he or she would like help with. The chores and problems might include cooking dinner, cleaning the house, doing homework, writing letters, or sorting the trash into recycling bins. Pitch in, and give each person a hand. Talk about the difference between cooperating and going it alone. How does it feel to know your family will give you a helping hand when you ask for it?

Permission to photocopy this handout from Group's Hands-On Bible Curriculum™ for Grades 1 and 2 granted for local church use. Copyright © Group Publishing, Inc., P.O. Box 481, Loveland, CO 80539.

C·O·M·F·O·R·T A
F·R·I·E·N·D

THE POINT
Good friends comfort each other when they're sad.

THE BIBLE BASIS:

1 Samuel 20:24-42. David and Jonathan weep when David must leave.

Jonathan had tried everything he could think of to protect his good friend David from King Saul's obsessive desire to destroy him. But finally, Jonathan and David realized that the only way for David to stay alive was for him to flee from Saul. The two friends were heartbroken. When David fled from Saul, it meant leaving behind his best friend. And in the violent circumstances, it was unlikely that they would ever regain the closeness that they'd had.

When bad things happen, it's easy to feel that we face them all alone. But it doesn't have to be that way. God wants us to be compassionate with each other. It's not enough that we enjoy our friends during good times. The true test of friendship is how loyal we are during bad times. Even children can be comforting and compassionate with their friends. Instinctively, they *feel* bad for their friends. But they need help to know what to *do* when their friends are hurting. Use this lesson to teach children how to be good friends when their friends are hurting.

Other Scriptures used in this lesson are **Romans 12:15; 2 Corinthians 1:3-4;** and **Galatians 6:2.**

KEY VERSE
for Lessons 9–13

"…live in harmony with one another; be sympathetic, love as brothers, be compassionate and humble" (1 Peter 3:8).

GETTING THE POINT

Children will

- talk about the things that make their friends sad,
- learn to comfort each other with the same kind of comfort they receive from God, and
- make a craft to cheer up a sad friend.

Before the lesson, collect the items from the Learning Lab for the activities you plan to use. Refer to the pictures in the margin to see what each item looks like.

THIS LESSON AT A GLANCE

SECTION	MINUTES	WHAT CHILDREN WILL DO	LEARNING LAB SUPPLIES	CLASSROOM SUPPLIES
WELCOME TIME	up to 5	**Welcome!**—Receive a warm welcome from the teacher and make name tags.		"Best Friends Name Tags" (p. 115), scissors, markers, tape or safety pins
ATTENTION GRABBER	up to 10	**Beat Up**—Pretend to beat up the paper globe and talk about words, actions, and situations that hurt others.	Paper globe, dart blower, darts	Paper, scissors, tape
BIBLE EXPLORATION & APPLICATION	up to 10	**David Leaves**—Interact during the story from 1 Samuel 20:24-42 about David and Jonathan comforting each other.		Bible
	up to 10	**Soft and Fuzzy**—Talk about things that are soft and comforting, hear 2 Corinthians 1:3-4, and share God's comfort.	Hand puppet	Bible
	up to 15	**Pillow Comfort**—Make pillows to comfort their friends and learn from Galatians 6:2 that they can help each other with their troubles.	Flower foam	Bible, "Hug-a-Bear" handouts (p. 143), markers, scissors, construction paper, stapler
CLOSING	up to 10	**Everything's Better With a Friend**—Hear Romans 12:15, link arms with classmates, and sing a song to show they'll rejoice with and comfort their friends.	Cassette: "Everything's Better With a Friend," "Lyrics Poster"	Bible, cassette player

Remember to make photocopies of the "Growing Together" handout (p. 144) to send home with your children. "Growing Together" is a valuable tool for helping first- and second-graders talk with their parents about what they're learning in class.

T·H·E L·E·S·S·O·N

 WELCOME TIME

WELCOME!
(up to 5 minutes)

- Greet each child individually with an enthusiastic smile.
- Thank each child for coming to class today.
- As children arrive, ask them about last week's "Growing Together" discussion. Use questions such as "What chores or problems did you help members of your family with last week?" and "Were you able to work out a problem with a friend last week? What happened?"
- Say: **Today we're going to learn that ✦ good friends comfort each other when they're sad.**

THE POINT ✦

- Hand out the name tags children made during Lesson 9, and help them attach the name tags to their clothing. If some of the name tags were damaged, or if children weren't in class that week, have them make new name tags using the photocopiable handout on page 115.
- Tell the children that the attention-getting signal you'll use during this lesson is clapping your hands three times. Ask children to respond by clapping their hands three times as they stop talking and focus their attention on you. Rehearse the signal with the children, telling them to respond quickly so you'll have plenty of time for all the fun activities planned for this lesson.

 ATTENTION GRABBER

 **LEARNING LAB**

BEAT UP
(up to 10 minutes)

Give each child a small rectangle of paper about the size of an index card. Have children roll up their slips of paper into tubes and tape them.

Have children line up shoulder to shoulder then sit down. Inflate the *paper globe,* and put it on the floor about 10 feet in front of the children. Have children take turns blowing *darts* with the *dart blower* at the *paper globe.* Avoid

spreading germs by having children insert their paper tubes inside the opening of the *dart blower*. They can blow through the paper instead of putting their mouths on the plastic. Continue playing until everyone has had at least one turn and the *paper globe* has been hit several times.

Then retrieve the *dart blower, darts,* and *paper globe* and return them to the Learning Lab. Have children throw away their paper tubes. Ask:

● **Our *paper globe* looked pretty sad—what makes you sad?** (When sad things happen on television; getting sick; being left out.)

● **If this *paper globe* were a person and it had feelings, how do you think it would have felt when the class ganged up on it?** (Bad; it would hurt from being hit so much; it would feel left out.)

● **If I had been the *paper globe*, I would have been afraid. What makes you afraid?** (Storms; bad guys who hurt people; weird noises at night.)

● **What makes you feel better when you're sad or afraid?** (My mom comes and hugs me; being with my friends; praying to God.)

Say: **Everyone gets scared and sad sometimes. It's great to have friends and family members to help us.**  **Good friends comfort each other when they're sad or afraid. Let's find out about two friends who were very sad and what they did to comfort each other.**

BIBLE EXPLORATION & APPLICATION

DAVID LEAVES 📖

(up to 10 minutes)

Open your Bible to **1 Samuel 20:24-42,** and show children the passage. Keep your Bible open in front of you. Say: **Last time, we learned about the plan that David and Jonathan came up with to save David from Saul. This time, let's find out what happened.**

David hid in the field just as he and Jonathan had planned. Let's pretend we're hiding. Cover your head with your hands, and make yourself very small. Pause.

Jonathan went to the festival and sat across from his father at the banquet table. But David's place at the table remained empty. Let's pretend that we're eating at the banquet. Pause.

Saul asked, "Why hasn't David come to the festival?"

Jonathan said: "David begged to go to Bethlehem to be with his family for the festival. That's why he's not here."

Saul was very angry. He said to Jonathan: "Bring David to me. He must die!" Let's pound our fists into the palms of our hands to show how angry Saul was. Pause.

★ **THE POINT**

But Jonathan said: "Why should David be killed? He hasn't done anything wrong!"

Saul was so angry that he picked up his spear and threw it at Jonathan! Let's pretend we're dodging the spear. Move quickly out of the way. Pause.

Jonathan escaped and left the table. He was ashamed of his father and upset because he knew his father still wanted to kill David. Let's cover our faces to show how sad Jonathan was. Pause.

The next morning Jonathan went to the field to meet David as they had agreed. He shot an arrow out into the field. Let's pretend to shoot an arrow. Pause. Then he said to the boy who had come with him: "The arrow is far beyond you. Hurry! Go quickly! Don't stop!" Jonathan called out to warn David to run away, because Saul was determined to kill him. Cup your hands around your mouth as if you're calling. Pause.

After the boy had picked up the arrow and given it to Jonathan, Jonathan sent him back to town. David came out from his hiding place. He hugged Jonathan for being such a good friend. Hug someone close to you. Pause. Then they both cried because they were so sad. David and Jonathan knew that they wouldn't see each other again. Rub your eyes, and pretend to cry. Pause.

Jonathan said to David, "Go in peace. We've promised to be good friends. God will be with us and with our children."

Then David left, and Jonathan went back to town. Ask:

● **Have you ever moved away from a good friend, or has a good friend ever moved away from you? How did you feel when that happened?** (Bad; terrible; sad.)

● **Did people comfort you? What did they do?** (My mom took me to visit my friend; my father hugged me; my friend sent me a letter.)

● **How did Jonathan and David comfort each other?** (They hugged; they promised to always be friends.)

Say: **David and Jonathan were very sad because they wouldn't see each other again. They comforted each other by hugging, crying together, and promising to be friends forever. It's good to comfort each other.** ✦ **Good friends always comfort each other when they're sad.** Let's find out why.

Teacher Tip
Some kids may not feel comfortable hugging others in class. That's OK. Let those kids shake hands with other class members instead.

THE POINT ★

SOFT AND FUZZY 📖
(up to 10 minutes)

LEARNING LAB

Have children sit on the floor. Put the *hand puppet* in your lap, and stroke it as if you were stroking a pet. Say: **When I'm sad, I feel comforted when I touch something soft and warm. When I pass this soft puppet around, pet it with your hand or rub it on your cheek. Then tell us one thing that comforts you when you're sad.** Pass the puppet around the circle to

"...live in harmony with one another; be sympathetic, love as brothers, be compassionate and humble" (1 Peter 3:8).

Family is still foremost in young children's lives, and nothing is as comforting to them as home. Show children that friends can offer and receive the kind of comfort that's usually found only in families.

THE POINT

Teacher Tip

If you have a large class, have children stuff their pillows with tissues or paper towels.

the right, and have children mention ideas such as "hugs," "hot chocolate," and "smiles from friends."

When the puppet comes back to you, say: **Listen to what the Bible says about getting and giving comfort. Be ready to tell me where comfort comes from first.** Read **2 Corinthians 1:3-4.** Ask:

● **Where does comfort come from first?** (From God.)

● **How does God comfort you?** (God helps me when I'm scared; God lets me know that he's there; God tells me he loves me.)

Say: **Let's comfort each other with the comfort we've received.**

Rub the puppet on your own arm, and say: **God gives me comfort because he promises to be with me all the time.**

To the child on your left say: **God gives me comfort when I'm sad, and I'll comfort you when you're sad.** Rub the puppet on his or her arm. Then have that child rub the puppet on the next child's arm and say, "God gives me comfort when I'm sad, and I'll comfort you when you're sad."

Continue until the puppet comes back to you.

Say: **Everyone here is a good friend—you've shown each other comfort, and you've received comfort just as it says in the Bible.** Read **2 Corinthians 1:3-4** again. ✦ **Good friends comfort each other when they're sad.**

Return the *hand puppet* to the Learning Lab.

PILLOW COMFORT 📖

(up to 15 minutes)

Photocopy a "Hug-a-Bear" handout (p. 143) for each child.

Say: **Now we know that comfort softens the sadness our friends feel and helps them feel better. Listen to what the Bible says about helping each other.** Read **Galatians 6:2** aloud. **Let's help our friends with their troubles by making something that will soften their sadness.**

Give each child a "Hug-a-Bear" handout. Have children cut out their bears and use markers to decorate them. Then have them trace around their handouts on construction paper and cut out the tracings. Have children each put their two bears together and staple all the way around them, leaving an opening in the top.

Divide the *flower foam* among the children, and have them cut it into pieces and stuff the pieces inside the bears. Then help the children staple the tops of

Bring in fabric scraps, and have children trace the bear handout onto the fabric to make soft pillows to give to their friends.

the bears to make pillows. Ask:

● **How would you feel if you got a bear like this when you were sad?** (I'd feel better; good, because I'd know that someone cared about me.)

● **How do you think your friend will feel when you give the bear to him or her?** (Good; better.)

● **Why do you want to make your friend feel better?** (Because I love my friend; I care for my friend; God says to comfort others.)

Say: **Friends are special. God wants us to treat our friends with love. Each of you can be a true, comforting friend. ✦ Good friends comfort each other when they're sad. Give these bears to your friends to comfort them.**

THE POINT

We believe that Christian education extends beyond the classroom into the home. Photocopy the "Growing Together" handout (p. 144) for this week, and send it home with your children. Encourage children and parents to use the handout to plan meaningful activities on this week's topic. Follow up the "Growing Together" activities next week by asking children what their families did together.

CLOSING

EVERYTHING'S BETTER WITH A FRIEND 📖

(up to 10 minutes)

Ask:

● **What did you learn today?** (I learned to be nice to my friends when they're sad; I learned to comfort my friends.)

Say: **Listen to what the Bible says we should do for our friends.** Read **Romans 12:15.** Ask:

● **What should we do for our friends?** (Be happy with them; be sad with them.)

Say: **To show that we want to rejoice with our friends and comfort our friends, let's link arms.** Have children stand in a circle and link arms.

Choose a volunteer to hold the "Lyrics Poster." Choose another volunteer to point to the words as children sing them.

Sing "Everything's Better With a Friend" with the *cassette tape.* Have the class

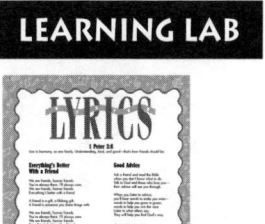

**THE POINT**

sway back and forth in time with the music. Then pray: **God, thank you for giving us good friends. And thank you for giving us comfort to make us feel better. Help us to comfort our friends because ★ good friends comfort each other when they're sad. In Jesus' name, amen.**

I'm praying this bear will soften your sadness.

FRIENDSHIP 12:

Good friends comfort each other when they're sad.

KEY VERSE

"...live in harmony with one another; be sympathetic, love as brothers, be compassionate and humble" (1 Peter 3:8).

GROWING TOGETHER

Permission to photocopy this handout from Group's Hands-On Bible Curriculum™ for Grades 1 and 2 granted for local church use. Copyright © Group Publishing, Inc., P.O. Box 481, Loveland, CO 80539.

I·N T·O·U·C·H

Today your child learned how to comfort a friend who's sad. The children learned that everyone gets sad and that God wants us to be kind to each other and help each other through tough times. Use these activities at home to teach your child what to do to ease someone's sadness.

LONG-LASTING COMFORT
....

Sometimes kids need something comforting—like this pillowcase—to hold all night long. Buy one yard of fake-fur fabric. Fold it the long way with the furry part on the inside. Stitch across one short end and up the long side, one-half inch from the edge of the fabric. Fold back the opening of the open side one-half inch, and stitch the edge down all the way around the pillowcase. Turn right side out, and stuff a pillow inside.

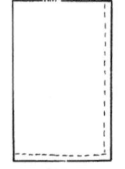 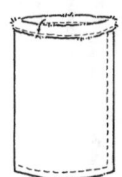 

COMFORT PACKAGE
....

Make a comfort package for a friend who's sad. Include packets of hot chocolate or hot apple-cider mix, a package of cookies, clippings of comic strips from the newspaper, and a card that includes 2 Thessalonians 2:16-17, "May our Lord Jesus Christ himself and God our Father, who loved us and by his grace gave us eternal encouragement and good hope, encourage your hearts and strengthen you in every good deed and word."

CHEERY CRANBERRY SAUCE
....

This cheery cranberry sauce is easy to make! You'll need 1 pound of cranberries, 1 cup of sugar, and a large pot. Your child will enjoy testing the berries for freshness—good cranberries will bounce on a table top. Throw away any that don't bounce. Put the sugar and 1 cup of water in the pot, and cook over medium heat until it boils. Add berries, and cook for 15 minutes, stirring frequently. Put the handle of the pan toward the back of the stove so the pot doesn't get knocked over. Supervise while your child carefully helps you stir the mixture. Pour the mixture into a pretty bowl (you can strain out the berries if you wish), and chill until you're ready to eat. Talk about things that are cheery—things that could help a sad person be happy.

THANKSGIVING POEMS
....

Thinking about what you're thankful for can be comforting because it reassures your faith in a gracious God. Before your Thanksgiving meal, have each family member write the word "THANKFUL" vertically on a piece of paper. Then have your family members each think of something they're thankful for that begins with each letter. For example, you might be thankful for <u>T</u>ea, <u>H</u>osannas, <u>A</u>nimals, <u>N</u>eedlework, <u>K</u>infolk, <u>F</u>lowers, <u>U</u>mbrellas, and <u>L</u>ove.

G·O·D I·S O·U·R
F·R·I·E·N·D

THE POINT
God wants to be our friend.

THE BIBLE BASIS:
2 Samuel 2:1-7; 7:1-16. God is a friend to David.

David had a remarkable relationship with God. And thanks to David's psalms, we have an emotion-filled record of their relationship. God was a faithful friend to David. He took care of David and made him victorious over his enemies. He gave David power, wisdom, and the love of the people. David was blessed with great riches. God held no gift back from David, except for the opportunity to build a permanent dwelling place for the ark of the covenant—and even then God promised that David's son would build it. While David wasn't perfect, he was faithful to God. David was quick to praise God and give him honor. He sought God with his whole heart. He loved God with a burning intensity.

That's the kind of friendship that God wants with each of us. It's hard for first- and second-graders to comprehend that God wants to be included in every day of their lives in the same way a best friend is involved in their lives. Teach your students that God is the best friend they'll ever have—he watches over them, protects them, loves them, and will be with them always. Show them that God desires friendship with them so much that he sent his Son so they could have a relationship with him.

Other Scriptures used in this lesson are **Joshua 1:5; Psalm 32:8;** and **John 3:16.**

KEY VERSE
for Lessons 9–13

"…live in harmony with one another; be sympathetic, love as brothers, be compassionate and humble" (1 Peter 3:8).

GETTING THE POINT

Children will

- discover that God watches over them because he wants to be their friend,
- learn that God sent Jesus so they could be friends with God, and
- talk about what they can do to be God's friends.

Before the lesson, collect the items from the Learning Lab for the activities you plan to use. Refer to the pictures in the margin to see what each item looks like.

THIS LESSON AT A GLANCE

SECTION	MINUTES	WHAT CHILDREN WILL DO	LEARNING LAB SUPPLIES	CLASSROOM SUPPLIES
WELCOME TIME	up to 5	**Welcome!**—Receive a warm welcome from the teacher and make name tags.		"Best Friends Name Tags" (p. 115), scissors, markers, tape or safety pins
ATTENTION GRABBER	up to 10	**I Spy**—Play I Spy and learn that God watches over them and protects them all the time.	Dart blower	Bible
BIBLE EXPLORATION & APPLICATION	up to 10	**God Is David's Friend**—Listen to a story from 2 Samuel 2:1-7 and 7:1-16 to learn that God was a friend to David.	Feather ball	Bible
	up to 10	**Mirror Images**—Mimic each other's actions, follow each other, and learn from Joshua 1:5 that God will be with them all the time.		Bible
	up to 15	**God's Friendship Gift**—Learn from John 3:16 that God sent Jesus because he wanted to be friends with us, talk about the good things that Jesus did, and thank God for his gift of friendship.	Learning Lab box, foam person, glitter pins	Bible, flat paper crown, tape
CLOSING	up to 10	**God Is a Forever Friend**—Talk about ways to be God's friend and sing a song as a promise to be friends with God.	Cassette: "Everything's Better With a Friend," "Lyrics Poster"	Cassette player

Remember to make photocopies of the "Growing Together" handout (p. 153) to send home with your children. "Growing Together" is a valuable tool for helping first- and second-graders talk with their parents about what they're learning in class.

T·H·E L·E·S·S·O·N

WELCOME TIME

WELCOME!
(up to 5 minutes)

- Greet each child individually with an enthusiastic smile.
- Thank each child for coming to class today.
- As children arrive, ask them about last week's "Growing Together" discussion. Use questions such as "How did you comfort someone who was sad last week?" and "In what ways does God comfort you?"
- Say: **Today we're going to learn that ★ God wants to be our friend.**

- Hand out the name tags children made during Lesson 9, and help them attach the name tags to their clothing. If some of the name tags were damaged, or if children weren't in class that week, have them make new name tags using the photocopiable handout on page 115.
- Tell the children that the attention-getting signal you'll use during this lesson is clapping your hands three times. Ask children to respond by clapping their hands three times as they stop talking and focus their attention on you. Rehearse the signal with the children, telling them to respond quickly so you'll have plenty of time for all the fun activities planned for this lesson.

MODULE REVIEW

Use the casual interaction time at the beginning of class to ask children the following module-review questions:
- **How have you depended on a good friend recently?**
- **When have you been happy for a friend during the past few weeks?**
- **What problem did you work out with a friend lately?**
- **How did you comfort a friend recently?**
- **What's your favorite thing you've learned this month? Why?**

ATTENTION GRABBER

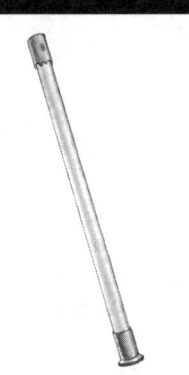
LEARNING LAB

I SPY 📖

(up to 10 minutes)

Have children sit in a circle. Give a volunteer the *dart blower,* and have the children play I Spy. Tell the volunteer to look through the *dart blower* and "spy" something. Tell the rest of the children to ask yes-and-no questions to help them guess what was spied. Whoever guesses what was spied gets to look through the *dart blower* and choose another item. Play several rounds. Then put the *dart blower* away, and ask:

● **How much of the room could you see through the *dart blower?*** (Not very much; only one thing at time; only small things.)

Say: **We could see only a little bit of the room when we looked through the *dart blower.* That works out fine for the game I Spy because you need to spot only one thing at a time. But God can see everything all at once. He watches everything that happens. Listen to what the Bible says.** Read **Psalm 32:8.** Ask:

● **Why does God watch over you?** (To show me where to go; to see if I do good things or bad things; to protect me; because he loves me.)

● **When does God watch over you?** (Always; at night when I'm sleeping; when I do something bad.)

Say: **We can see only a little bit of what happens in the world. It's like looking through the *dart blower.* We can see only a small part of the room at once. But God can see everything that happens in the entire world. That's good, because God watches over us to protect us and take care of us. God watches over us all the time because he loves us.** ★ **God wants to be our friend. God will be the best friend you'll ever have. Let's find out how God was David's good friend.**

Teacher Tip

It's important to say The Point just as it's written in each activity. Repeating The Point over and over will help children remember it and apply it to their lives.

★ **THE POINT**

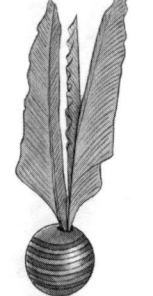
LEARNING LAB

 BIBLE EXPLORATION & APPLICATION

GOD IS DAVID'S FRIEND 📖

(up to 10 minutes)

Open your Bible to **2 Samuel 2:1-7** and **7:1-16,** and show the passages to the children. Say: **Today's story tells how God was a faithful friend to**

David. We're going to use the *feather ball* to help tell the story because it shows us what "faithful" means. When you toss the ball against a wall, it will always flip around in the air and return to you with the ball first and the feathers trailing behind. God is faithful because he always does what he says he'll do.

Have children sit in a row about 10 feet away from a classroom wall. Sit to the side of them. Give the first child the *feather ball*. Say: **Listen carefully to the story. When you hear about a friendly thing that God did for David, toss the ball against the wall. Catch the ball, and give it to the next person in line. Everyone listen carefully. If you hear about a friendly thing that God does, encourage whoever's holding the ball to toss it. Here we go!**

As you tell this story, pause to indicate that the children should toss the ball. There are 12 pauses in the story. If you have more than 12 children in your class, have the remaining children each think of a friendly thing God has done for them then toss the ball.

Say: **When King Saul died, God made David king over Judah just as he had promised.** Pause. **Then God made David's kingdom peaceful—David's enemies no longer attacked the country.** Pause.

One day, David said to Nathan the prophet, "God has given me a beautiful palace to live in that's made of sweet-smelling cedar wood. Pause. **But the ark of the covenant is in a tent! God has been kind to me by giving me so much. I should build a beautiful temple for the ark of the covenant."**

That night, God gave a message to Nathan to give to David. God said, "You were a shepherd who took care of sheep. But I made you king—the leader of my people. Pause. **I have been with you everywhere you have gone.** Pause. **I have defeated your enemies for you.** Pause. **I will make you as famous as any of the great people in the world.** Pause. **I will continue to give you peace from your enemies.** Pause. **Your children and your grandchildren will be kings of Israel after you.** Pause.

When you die, one of your sons will become the next king. Pause. **He's the one who will build a temple for the ark of the covenant. I will never stop loving your son.** Pause. **Someone from your family will be king forever."** Pause.

Nathan told David everything that God had said. Then David praised God. He said, "You have made wonderful promises about me and my family. You have already given me so many good things. You are a great God! There is no one else like you."

Put the *feather ball* back in the Learning Lab. Ask:

● **Why was God a good friend to David?** (Because he loved David; because God is a good friend to everyone.)

● **How does God show that he's a good friend to you?** (He promises to love me all the time; God stays with me; God protects me; God gave me a good family.)

Say: ✦ **God wants to be our friend, just as he was a friend to David. God always keeps his promises to us, just as he kept his promises to David. Let's find out what else God does for us.**

BIBLE INSIGHT

David's palace of cedar timbers was built in Jerusalem, the city of David, on the eastern slope of Mount Zion. This strategic location gave him both military strength and political power, since the site was essentially "neutral." And when David moved the ark of the covenant to the city, he made Jerusalem the religious capital of the nation. In the Old Testament, the city of David refers to Jerusalem; in the New Testament, it refers to Bethlehem.

THE POINT ★

MIRROR IMAGES 📖

(up to 10 minutes)

Form pairs. Have partners take turns shadowing each other. Have partners stand facing each other and choose which one will go first. That partner will make motions and faces, and the other partner will copy the actions. After one minute, have partners switch roles. After another minute, call time by blowing the *balloon squawker.* Have children sit together on the floor. Ask:

● **Was it easy or difficult to shadow your partner? Explain.** (Easy, my partner did his motions slowly so I could follow them; hard, I couldn't figure out what my partner was going to do; hard, I was laughing too hard to follow my partner.)

Say: **It's hard to stick with our partners even when we do our best to imitate them. But God doesn't have any trouble sticking with us. No matter what we do, God sticks with us all the time. Listen to what the Bible says about God.** Read **Joshua 1:5.** Ask:

● **What does God promise to do?** (Always be with us; never leave us.)

Say: **Let's see what it would be like to always be with someone. Stand by your partner. Choose one partner to be in front and one partner to be in back. If you're the back partner, put your hands on your partner's waist. Front partners, lead your back partners around the room, and see if they can stick with you.**

Have the children in front lead their partners around the room in a fast-paced, winding way. After a minute or two, have the children switch roles. After another minute or two, blow into the *balloon squawker* to get children's attention. Have the children sit down. Ask:

● **Was it easy to lead your partner? Was it easy to follow? Explain.** (Easy, because she followed so well; hard, because I didn't know where he was going.)

● **How was this like the way God stays with us? How was it different?** (God stays close to us; God doesn't stay behind us; God lives inside of us.)

Say: **God stays with us all the time and will never leave us no matter how fast we go or where we go. God wants to lead us and guide us—to show us the right way to go. God will always be with us to protect us and guide us because ★ God wants to be our friend.**

Return the *balloon squawker* to the Learning Lab.

 **THE POINT**

GOD'S FRIENDSHIP GIFT 📖

(up to 15 minutes)

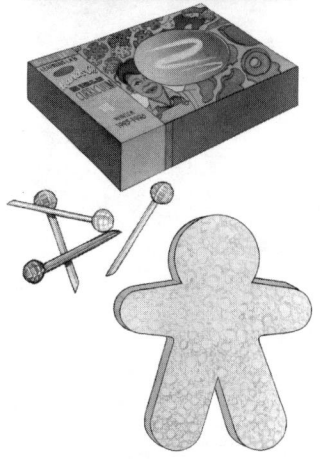

Take all of the items out of the Learning Lab box except the *foam person* and *glitter pins*. Attach a flat paper crown to the head of the *foam person*. Gather the children in a circle. Place the box on your lap, but don't let the children see inside it.

Say: **Sometimes friends give gifts to each other. I have something inside this box that represents a gift that God has given to each of you to show his love and friendship for you. Listen to this Bible verse, and see if you know what the gift is.** Read **John 3:16.** Ask:

● **What is the gift that God has given to you?** (His Son; Jesus; everlasting life.)

Open the box, and show children the *foam person* and *glitter pins.* Say: **God loves you very much.** ✦ **God wants to be our friend. That's why God sent Jesus to the world. Jesus did wonderful things while he was here, but the best thing Jesus did was to die on the cross for the wrong things we have done. Because Jesus died on the cross for our sins, we can live with God and be God's friend forever.**

Once, some men made Jesus wear a crown of prickly thorns. But Jesus deserves to wear a glittery crown full of beautiful jewels. We're going to make Jesus a glittery crown to say thank you for being such a good friend to us.

Let's think of the good things that Jesus did to show that he wanted to be our good friend. For each idea you have, take a *glitter pin*, and stick it into the crown on the head of the *foam person*. When we're finished, it will look like a crown full of precious jewels.

Have children think of the good things Jesus did, such as dying on the cross, healing sick people, and feeding hungry people. For each idea, let children stick a *glitter pin* in the crown.

Say: **Let's thank God for being such a good friend that he sent Jesus. Let's all say, "Thank you, God, for sending Jesus to us."** Pause.

Then take a *glitter pin* out of the crown, and pin it to a small slip of paper. Say: **This is to remind you of God's friendship.** Continue to remove pins from the crown, and give them to the children to take home.

THE POINT ✦

KEY VERSE Connection

"...live in harmony with one another; be sympathetic, love as brothers, be compassionate and humble" (1 Peter 3:8).

Teach your young children that because of Jesus, we can be close to God—the ultimate friend! Use the Key Verse to show children how to model friendship to each other.

CLOSING

GOD IS A FOREVER FRIEND

(up to 10 minutes)

Ask:
● **What did you learn today?** (God watches me; God is always with me; God wants to be my friend.)
● **What can you do to show you'll be friends with God?** (Spend time with God; tell others about God; sing songs to God.)

Say: **Great ideas! Let's sing "Everything's Better With a Friend" as a promise to be God's friend. While we sing, think about what you'll do this week to be God's friend.**

Choose a volunteer to hold the "Lyrics Poster." Choose another volunteer to point to the words as you sing them. Play the tape, and sing along. When the song is over, turn off the cassette player, and pray: **God, ★ we know you want to be our friend. You promised to watch over us and be with us. You sent your Son, Jesus, so that we can be your friends. Help us be good friends to you. Thank you for being our friend. In Jesus' name, amen.**

FRIENDSHIP 13:

God wants to be our friend.

KEY VERSE

"...live in harmony with one another; be sympathetic, love as brothers, be compassionate and humble" (1 Peter 3:8).

GROWINGTOGETHER

Permission to photocopy this handout from Group's Hands-On Bible Curriculum™ for Grades 1 and 2 granted for local church use. Copyright © Group Publishing, Inc., P.O. Box 481, Loveland, CO 80539.

I·N T·O·U·C·H

Today your child learned that God wants to be our friend. The children learned that God watches over them, protects them, and stays with them. The children also learned that God gave Jesus, a precious gift, so that they could be friends with him. Use these activities to teach your child about friendship and how to be a friend to God.

PIZZA AND FRIENDS

· · · · · · · ·

Invite several of your child's friends over for an after-Thanksgiving pizza party. Give each child half an English muffin. Provide pizza sauce, cheddar cheese, mozzarella cheese, Parmesan cheese, and lots of different pizza toppings. Let each child top his or her own pizza. Put the pizzas on a baking sheet, and bake at 375° for about 10 minutes or until the cheese is bubbly. Don't forget to thank God for friendship and good food before you eat.

SWEET-SMELLING FRIENDSHIP

· · · · · · · · · · ·

Put several drops of vanilla flavoring inside a deflated balloon. Be careful not to let any of the flavoring touch the outside of the balloon. Blow up the balloon just enough to allow it to fit inside a shoe box. Place the balloon inside the box, and put the lid on tightly. Leave it closed for an hour. Open the box, and you'll smell vanilla. Talk with your child about God's love. Say, "The material the balloon is made of isn't strong or thick enough to keep the sweet smell of the vanilla inside. God's love is like the sweet vanilla. It's so strong and powerful that there's nothing that can separate us from God's love." Read Romans 8:37-39 together.

MUSICAL RIDDLE

· · · · · · · · · ·

Sing this song for your child to the tune of "Did You Ever See a Lassie?" See who your child would name as a great friend. If your child doesn't think of it, remind him or her that God is a great friend.

> Did you ever have a friend
> Who was caring and loving?
> This great friend is like no other.
> Do you know who he is?

FRIENDSHIP SUN-CATCHER

· · · · · · · · · · ·

Create a cheery sun-catcher by taping colored tissue paper shapes to the

window in a design that will remind you of God's friendship. Every time the sun shines through the tissue, thank God for his friendship.

PARENT TIP

· · · · · · · · · ·

Teach your children John 15:14, "You are my friends if you do what I command." Then, when you remind your children to obey God's rules, motivate them by explaining that we follow God's rules because we love God. Obeying God is a way to praise God with our lives. You might want to call God's rules "love commands" or "friendship rules" to remind your children to live as God's friends.

B·O·N·U·S
I·D·E·A·S

GREAT GAMES

DAVID'S JOURNEY

Form two teams. Set up identical courses for each team, and have them speed walk through the course as they would a relay race. Here are the obstacles:

Obstacle 1: Taking Care of Sheep—Place a piece of paper one-fourth of the way through the course. Children must stand on this square and "baa" three times before moving on.

Obstacle 2: Saul's Harp—Place a second piece of paper halfway through the course. Children must sit on the paper and hum "Jesus Loves Me" as they strum an imaginary harp.

Obstacle 3: Saul's Spear—Place a chair three-fourths of the way through the course. Children must jump down behind the chair to avoid Saul's spear, then pop up to continue the race.

Obstacle 4: Saul's Chase—Place another chair at the end of the course. Children must walk around the chair three times to escape Saul in the wilderness, then go back to the beginning, where the next child starts the course.

This game works well with Lessons 5 through 8 on David.

MANERFISH TAG

Choose a child to be a "manerfish"—a manerfish is the opposite of a fisherman. The manerfish must catch all of the people in your class by squirting them with the *squirty fish* from the Learning Lab. Provide a bucket of water for refills. Once a person is squirted, he or she must drop to a sitting position on the floor (which is the water) and make swimming motions until everyone else is caught. The last person caught is the next manerfish.

This game works well with any lesson in this book.

GOLF

Make a masking tape line. Set one of the *plastic rings* five feet away from the line. Set the second ring seven feet away. Continue setting each ring a couple of feet farther away from the line. Use the *dart blower* as a golf club and the *super bouncing wheel* as a golf ball, and have children try to gently putt the wheel onto the *plastic ring*. The wheel must touch the ring, but still counts as a "hole" even if it passes over the ring. As soon as everyone has touched the ring, take the first *plastic ring* away, and have children try to hit the second ring. Continue until everyone has golfed the "course."

This golf game works well with any lesson in this book.

FFIRMATION ACTIVITIES

HE'S GOT THE WHOLE WORLD IN HIS HANDS

Inflate the *paper globe*. Have the children sit in a circle and pass around the globe as they sing "He's Got the Whole World in His Hands." For the second verse, sing, "He's got my friend _____ in his hands," and toss the globe to that person. Let the chosen person name the next person to throw the ball to. Sing the third verse to him or her. Continue until everyone has had a turn. For the closing verse, sing:

He's got you and me, brother, in his hands.
He's got you and me, sister, in his hands.
He's got everybody here in his hands.
He's got the whole world in his hands.

FLOWERS OF GOOD DEEDS

Put a piece of *flower foam* on a photocopy machine, and make several photocopies. Cut apart the paper flowers, and write affirmations on them to hand out to the children. You might write, "I saw you share the markers today. Good job!" or "You were a good friend today when you worked out a problem with Seth. God is pleased with you."

Use these flower affirmations with any lesson in this book.

PUPPET AFFIRMATIONS

Put your hand inside the *hand puppet* to say goodbye to the children after class. Make the puppet gently peck the children's hands or nuzzle their cheeks. This works well with every lesson in this book.

FAITHFUL FRIENDS

Form pairs, and have the pairs line up, one pair behind another. Give the *feather ball* to the first pair in line. Have the partner who's holding the ball say, "I'll be your faithful friend" and throw the ball at the wall. Have the other partner catch the ball and say, "I'll be your faithful friend." Then have them give the ball to the next pair in line. Continue until all the partners have affirmed each other.

This activity works well with every lesson in this book.

ARTIES AND PROJECTS

THANKSGIVING PARTY

Say thank you to God with a party. Make paper chains out of brown and orange paper. For each loop, have children think of one thing they're thankful for. Play Turkey Tag: "It" is the hunter, and everyone else is a turkey. Have all the turkeys gobble until they're tagged. The last one tagged is the next hunter. Serve a harvest mix children will thank God for—candy corn, chocolate chips, fish crackers, peanuts, and pretzels.

FRIENDS FOREVER

Throw a party to celebrate friendship. Have children invite their best friends to the party. Before the party, make cardboard rectangles that are one inch bigger on all sides than an instant-print snapshot. As children arrive, take two pictures of each pair of best friends. Have children place the photos on the cardboard rectangles and decorate the edges with colored macaroni, sequins, glitter, rick-rack, or buttons. Play games that children play in pairs, such as three-legged races or wheelbarrow races. Give each set of best friends a root beer float with two straws and two spoons.

Try this celebration with Lessons 9 through 13 on friendship.

MAKE-A-COSTUME PARTY

Collect a variety of costume accessories such as old coats, wigs, and hats. Also provide clown makeup, paper grocery bags, construction paper, glue, paint, and other art supplies. When the children arrive, tell them that for this party they can pretend to be anyone they want to be. Have them design their own costumes, using the materials you've gathered. Have a costume fashion show. Take photos of each child. This party is a great alternative to a Halloween party. You can also use it to stress the importance of The Point in Lesson 5: God doesn't judge us by the way we look.

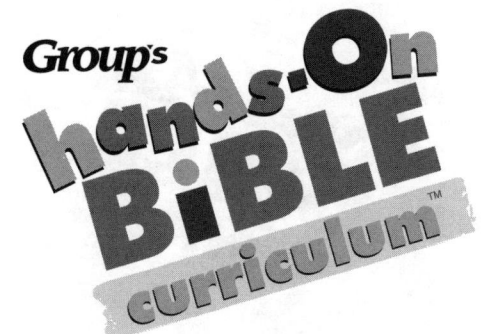

HOBC Marketing Survey

Please help Group Publishing continue to provide innovative and exciting resources to help your children know, love, and follow Christ. Take a moment to fill out and send back this survey. Thanks!

1. What level(s) of Hands-On Bible Curriculum™ are you using?

2. How many children are in your class? adult helpers?

3. How has the size of your class changed since using Hands-On Bible Curriculum?

❏ Remained the same ❏ Grown a lot
❏ Grown a little ❏ Other _____

Comments

4. When do you use Hands-On Bible Curriculum?

❏ Sunday school ❏ Midweek group
❏ Children's church ❏ Other (please describe) _____
_____
_____

5. What do you like best about the curriculum?

6. Is there anything about the curriculum you would like to see changed? (For example, if a certain lesson didn't work well, what specific changes would you recommend?)

7. What products would you like to see Group Publishing develop to fill specific needs in your church?

TEACH YOUR PRESCHOOLERS AS JESUS TAUGHT WITH GROUP'S *HANDS-ON BIBLE CURRICULUM*™

Hands-On Bible Curriculum™ for preschoolers helps your preschoolers learn the way they learn best—by touching, exploring, and discovering. With active learning, preschoolers love learning about the Bible, and they really remember what they learn.

Because small children learn best through repetition, Preschoolers and Pre-K & K will learn one important point per lesson, and Toddlers & 2s will learn one point each month with **Hands-On Bible Curriculum**. These important lessons will stick with them and comfort them during their daily lives. Your children will learn:

- God is our friend,
- who Jesus is, and
- we can always trust Jesus.

The **Learning Lab®** is packed with age-appropriate learning tools for fun, faith-building lessons. Toddlers & 2s explore big **Interactive StoryBoards™** with enticing textures that toddlers love to touch— like sandpaper for earth, cotton for clouds, and blue cellophane for water. **Bible Big Books™** captivate Preschoolers and Pre-K & K while teaching them important Bible lessons. With **Jumbo Bible Puzzles™** and involving **Learning Mats™**, your children will see, touch, and explore their Bible stories. Each quarter there's a brand new collection of supplies to keep your lessons fresh and involving.

Fuzzy, age-appropriate hand puppets are also available to add to the learning experience. These child-friendly puppets help you teach each lesson with scripts provided in the **Teachers Guide**. Plus, your children will enjoy teaching the puppets what they learned. Cuddles the Lamb, Whiskers the Mouse, and Pockets the Kangaroo turn each lesson into an interactive and entertaining learning experience.

Just order one **Learning Lab** and one **Teachers Guide** for each age level, add a few common classroom supplies, and presto—you have everything you need to build faith in your children. For more interactive fun, introduce your children to the age-appropriate puppet who will be your teaching assistant and their friend. **No student books are required!**

Hands-On Bible Curriculum is also available for grades 1–6.

Order today from your local Christian bookstore, or write: Group Publishing, P.O. Box 485, Loveland, CO 80539.